D0817756

Design for
Six Sigma

Other titles in the Briefcase Books series include:

Customer Relationship Management by Kristin Anderson and Carol Kerr

Communicating Effectively by Lani Arredondo

Performance Management by Robert Bacal

Recognizing and Rewarding Employees by R. Brayton Bowen

Motivating Employees by Anne Bruce and James S. Pepitone

Building a High Morale Workplace by Anne Bruce

Six Sigma for Managers by Greg Brue

Leadership Skills for Managers by Marlene Caroselli

Negotiating Skills for Managers by Steven P. Cohen

Effective Coaching by Marshall J. Cook

Conflict Resolution by Daniel Dana

Project Management by Gary R. Heerkens

Managing Teams by Lawrence Holpp

Hiring Great People by Kevin C. Klinvex, Matthew S. O'Connell, and Christopher P. Klinvex

Time Management by Marc Mancini

Retaining Top Employees by J. Leslie McKeown

Empowering Employees by Kenneth L. Murrell and Mimi Meredith

Presentation Skills for Managers by Jennifer Rotondo and Mike Rotondo

Finance for Non-Financial Managers by Gene Siciliano

The Manager's Guide to Business Writing by Suzanne D. Sparks

Skills for New Managers by Morey Stettner

The Manager's Survival Guide by Morey Stettner

Manager's Guide to Effective Meetings by Barbara J. Streibel

Interviewing Techniques for Managers by Carolyn P. Thompson

Managing Multiple Projects by Michael Tobis and Irene P. Tobis

To learn more about titles in the Briefcase Books series go to
www.briefcasebooks.com
You'll find the tables of contents, downloadable sample chapters, information on the authors, discussion guides for using these books in training programs, and more.

Design for Six Sigma

Greg Brue
Robert G. Launsby

McGraw-Hill

New York Chicago San Francisco Lisbon London
Madrid Mexico City Milan New Delhi San Juan
Seoul Singapore Sydney Toronto

The *McGraw-Hill* Companies

Copyright © 2003 by The McGraw-Hill Companies, Inc. All rights reserved.
Printed in the United States of America. Except as permitted under the
United States Copyright Act of 1976, no part of this publication may be
reproduced or distributed in any form or by any means, or stored in a database or retrieval system, without the prior written permission of the publisher.

2 3 4 5 6 7 8 9 0 AGM/AGM 0 9 8 7 6 5 4

ISBN 0-07-141376-6

Library of Congress Cataloging-in-Publication Data applied for.

This is a CWL Publishing Enterprises Book, *developed and produced for
McGraw-Hill by* CWL Publishing Enterprises. *For more information, contact
CWL Publishing Enterprises, Inc., 3010 Irvington Way, Madison, WI 53713,
www.cwlpub.com.*

This publication is designed to provide accurate and authoritative information in regard to the subject matter covered. It is sold with the understanding
that neither the author nor the publisher is engaged in rendering legal,
accounting, or other professional service. If legal advice or other expert
assistance is required, the services of a competent professional person
should be sought.
>   —From a Declaration of Principles jointly adopted by a Committee
>   of the American Bar Association and a Committee of Publishers

McGraw-Hill books are available at special quantity discounts to use as pre-
miums and sales promotions, or for use in corporate training programs. For
more information, please write to the Director of Special Sales, McGraw-Hill,
2 Penn Plaza, New York, NY 10128. Or contact your local bookstore.

 This book is printed on recycled, acid-free paper containing a minimum of 50% recycled de-inked fiber.

Contents

Preface   ix

1. **What Is Design for Six Sigma?**   1
   Six Sigma: The Basics   1
   Design for Six Sigma   4
   Design for Six Sigma Defined and Explained   8
   Myths About DFSS   10
   Manager's Checklist for Chapter 1   12

2. **Why Do Design for Six Sigma?**   14
   Why New Products and Services Fail   14
   DFSS and the Customer   16
   DFSS and Quality   17
   DFSS and Time   18
   DFSS and the Bottom Line   19
   Competitive Advantages   22
   More Than Just Tools   24
   Manager's Checklist for Chapter 2   26

3. **Core of Design for Six Sigma**   28
   The IDOV Method   32
   P—Plan/Prerequisites Phase   33
   I—Identify Phase   39
   D—Design Phase   46
   O—Optimize Phase   49
   V—Verify/Validate Phase   51
   The Basics by Any Name   52
   Manager's Checklist for Chapter 3   53

4. Design for Six Sigma Metrics — **54**
What Should You Measure? — 56
Standards — 58
Question Everything — 62
Measurement Reliability and Validity — 64
Financial Linkage of Metrics and Results — 66
Guidelines for Metrics — 66
Some Statistics — 72
Other Important Factors — 78
Conclusion — 78
Manager's Checklist for Chapter 4 — 79

5. People and Resources — **81**
Key Players and the DFSS Infrastructure — 81
Executive Leaders — 82
Champion — 84
Master Black Belt — 86
Black Belts — 88
Green Belts — 90
Team Members — 92
Teamwork — 94
Rewards and Recognition — 95
Consultants — 97
On to Implementing — 98
Manager's Checklist for Chapter 5 — 101

6. Implementing DFSS Successfully — **103**
CEOs and Executive Managers — 104
Executive Managers — 106
Executive Managers and Champions — 106
Champions — 108
Managers — 110
Obstacles — 111
Causes of Failure — 112
Recommendations — 115
Lessons Learned — 117
Manager's Checklist for Chapter 6 — 119

7. DFSS Tools, Part 1 — **120**
Phase-Gate Project Reviews — 121
Benchmarking — 123
Measurement System Analysis — 123
Voice of the Customer (VOC) — 125

Quality Function Deployment (QFD)   127
DFSS Scorecards   133
Pugh Concept Selection Technique   134
Design for X (DFx)   138
Manager's Checklist for Chapter 7   141

8. **DFSS Tools, Part 2**   **143**
Failure Modes and Effects Analysis (FMEA)   143
Anticipatory Failure Determination (AFD)   147
Poka-Yoke   148
Process Capability and Performance Studies   149
Multi-Vari Analysis   152
Design of Experiments (DOE)   154
Monte Carlo Simulation   157
Robust Design: Taguchi Methods   158
Tolerance Design and Tolerance Analysis   160
Control Plan   160
Tools, Tools, and More Tools   161
Manager's Checklist for Chapter 8   162

9. **How to Sustain Design for Six Sigma**   **164**
After 99.99966%, What Next?   164
Keeping the Capability   166
Keep the Customers in Mind and Involved   166
Make the Most of What You Know   167
Vision and Leadership   168
Infrastructure, Reinforcement, and Control   169
Organizational Culture   171
Into Every Area   176
Expanding DFSS Beyond the Organization   180
Manager's Checklist for Chapter 9   181

Index   **183**

Preface

DFSS is a business process focused on improving profitability. Properly applied, it generates the right product at the right time at the right cost. Through its use of product and team scorecards, it is a powerful program management technique.

DFSS is an enhancement to your new product development process, not a replacement for it. A documented, well-understood and useful new product development process is fundamental to a successful DFSS program.

Your new product development process provides the roadmap to success. DFSS provides tools and teamwork to get the job done in an efficient and effective manner. By rigorously applying the tools of DFSS you can be assured of predictable product quality.

DFSS provides a systematic integration of tools, methods, processes, and team members throughout product and process design.

For the majority of organizations, long-term success is tied directly to the new product development process. Tomorrow's revenue and growth are tightly bound to how successful you are at launching new products.

DFSS can serve as a mechanism to revolutionize the way you develop new products. To reap its benefits, you must be prepared to make major changes.

The size of the effort is formidable, but the payoff may be no smaller than company survival.
　　　　　—Charles Huber and Robert Launsby
　　　　　"Straight Talk on DFSS" (*Six Sigma Forum Magazine*, Vol. 1, No. 4, August 2002)

Design for Six Sigma (DFSS) is a systematic methodology for designing or redesigning products and/or services according to customer requirements and expectations. DFSS project teams integrate characteristics of Six Sigma at the outset of development with a disciplined set of tools, to achieve six sigma performance—a defect rate of 3.4 defects per million opportunities (DPMO), which is 99.9997% perfect.

DFSS is based on the belief that when you design Six Sigma quality into a product or a service, it's probable that customers will be satisfied with that product or service and your organization will benefit financially. By incorporating DFSS, you're virtually assured that your new product or service will perform well in the marketplace.

Although there are variations of DFSS, they all use a disciplined set of tools throughout the design process. Some of those tools will be familiar to you through your experiences with Six Sigma, but some are specific to DFSS. Similarly, the DFSS process, of which there are at least a half-dozen variations, is somewhat similar to the Six Sigma process of DMAIC (define, measure, analyze, improve, and control).

Is DFSS right for your organization? To answer that question, start by answering the following questions:

- How does your organization develop new products and services?
- What is the ratio of product or service failures to product or service successes in your organization?

Only about 60% of new products launched in all industries are a success and about 45% of resources allocated to developing and commercializing new products go into products that are killed or fail to provide adequate financial return. Companies gave the following reasons for the failure of new products (Robert G. Cooper, *Winning at New Products,* p. 25):

- inadequate market analysis: 24%
- product problems or defects: 16%

- lack of effective marketing effort: 14%
- higher costs than anticipated: 10%
- competitive strength or reaction: 9%
- poor timing of introduction: 8%
- technical or production problems: 6%

It's obvious that DFSS could help companies overcome many of the problems that cause new products to fail.

Chapter Highlights

Chapter 1 defines and explains Design for Six Sigma, examines its roots, and debunks some of the more influential myths that have developed around DFSS.

Chapter 2 is devoted to providing answers to the question, "Why do Design for Six Sigma?" It outlines the many advantages of applying Six Sigma principles and tools from the very start, to design products and services.

The core of DFSS is the subject of Chapter 3, which details the activities of each of the phases of this methodology, using as a model the PIDOV method (plan, identify, design, optimize, and verify). Although this method is the basis for our explanation of DFSS, what we say about it applies in general to the other versions, such as DMADV, DMADOV, DMCDOV, DCOV, DCCDI, DMEDI, and DMADIC. (Now you understand why we simplified by choosing only one method!)

Chapter 4 covers metrics, from general guidelines through standards, problems, and measurement to concepts and calculations—including the infamous "Six Sigma shift." It comes first after the basic introduction to DFSS because metrics constitute the scorecard for your DFSS projects: without the right metrics, you can't know how much progress you're making toward your goals.

Breaking away briefly from definitions, figures, phases, activities, and metrics, Chapter 5 gets to the heart of successful DFSS initiatives—the people. It lists the key players—executive leaders, champion, master black belt, black belts, green belts, and team members—and outlines qualifications, training and preparation, and roles and responsibilities. It closes with advice on working with consultants and then a short bibliography on DFSS and related subjects.

Chapter 6 provides guidelines and tips for implementing DFSS, from practitioners and consultants. This chapter may be relatively short, but the contents are vital to the success of your efforts.

With the foundation formed by the first six chapters, you're ready to get into the tools used by DFSS project teams. Chapters 7 and 8 present the most important of these tools, to the extent possible within the scope of this book.

Finally, the book concludes by offering recommendations for sustaining your DFSS efforts, "keeping the capability" by building on your successes and spreading the initiative throughout your organization and beyond.

From start to finish, this book is dedicated to one proposition—helping you apply Design for Six Sigma to your products and services from the start, where it's easiest and least expensive to achieve the highest levels of quality and performance and the greatest profitability.

Special Features

The idea behind the books in the Briefcase Series is to give you practical information written in a friendly, person-to-person style. The chapters are relatively short, deal with tactical issues, and include lots of examples. They also feature numerous boxes designed to give you different types of specific information. Here's a description of the boxes you'll find in this book.

These boxes do just what they say: give you tips and tactics for being smart in planning for and implementing Design for Six Sigma tools and techniques.

Smart
Managing

These boxes provide warnings for where things could go wrong when you're learning about and implementing Six Sigma techniques.

 These boxes give you how-to hints for undertaking the tools and techniques of Design for Six Sigma.

 Every subject has some special jargon and terms. These boxes provide definitions of these concepts.

 It's always useful to have examples of what others have done, either well or not so well. Find these stories in these boxes.

 This identifies boxes where you'll find specific procedures you can follow to take advantage of the book's advice.

 How can you make sure you won't make a mistake when implement DFSS? You can't, but these boxes will give you practical advice on how to minimize the possibility.

Acknowledgments

This book is a collaboration between the authors and CWL Publishing Enterprises, Inc., its developer. We especially want to thank Bob Magnan of CWL, who worked closely with us in pulling together the ideas that make up *Design for Six Sigma*. It would have been difficult to do this book without his help. We also want to thank John Woods, president of CWL for asking us to take on this project and Nancy Woods, also of CWL, who did the copyediting. I would be remiss if I didn't thank my wife Kelly for her encouragement and support throughout the course of this project. Finally, we want to thank you, our readers, for using this book to move your Six Sigma initiatives forward. We wish you good luck in your efforts.

About the Authors

Since 1994, **Greg Brue**, CEO of Six Sigma Consultants, Inc. and Master Black Belt, has implemented Six Sigma methodologies for some of the world's most recognized companies.

Greg trains Corporate Champions and mentors CEOs, senior executives, and company directors. A regular guest speaker at major business events and quality conferences, he also conducts Six Sigma seminars and monthly Executive Boot Camps. Greg supports numerous corporate Six Sigma implementations by maintaining direct contact with Black Belts, Master Black Belts, Champions, and senior managers.

Drawing on his considerable expertise, Greg developed the *Seven Principles of Problem-Solving Technology* to encapsulate and communicate the vision, purpose, and results of Six Sigma. As a result, he has been instrumental in changing the mindset and infrastructure at major corporations—empowering organizations to achieve significant measurable results. Experienced and expert Six Sigma practitioners, Greg and his team provide the corporate community with the vision, velocity and quantum gains required to decrease defects and increase profitability.

For more information about Six Sigma Consultants, visit www.sixsigmaco.com.

Bob Launsby is President of Launsby Consulting in Colorado Springs, Colorado. Since 1990, he has provided training and consulting in experimental design, problem solving, and Design For Six Sigma (DFSS). Clients include numerous large and small companies in the medical, automotive, computer and bio-medical community. He recently developed and launched Seagate's "DFSS for Marketing" seminar. Bob is the co-author of four books and developer of "DOE Wisdom" software. Visit his Web site at www.launsby.com.

What is Design for Six Sigma?

The best Six Sigma projects begin not inside the business but outside it, focused on answering the question, how can we make the customer more competitive?
—Jack Welch

Six Sigma: The Basics

Since you're reading this book, you're probably familiar with at least the basics of Six Sigma. So, we can review briefly before getting into Design for Six Sigma.

Six Sigma is a revolutionary business process geared toward dramatically reducing organizational inefficiencies that translates into bottom-line profitability. It started in the 1980s at Motorola; then, organizations such as GE, Allied Signal, and Seagate worked with the initiative during the 1990s and made it the most successful business initiative of the era.

Key to the Six Sigma methodology of the 1990s is a five-step process—Define, Measure, Analyze, Improve, and Control

(DMAIC). By systematically applying these steps (with the appropriate tools), practitioners of this approach have been able to save substantial dollars.

Six Sigma Defined and Explained

The basis of Six Sigma is measuring a process in terms of defects. The statistical concept of six sigma means your processes are working nearly perfectly, delivering only 3.4 defects per million opportunities (DPMO). As you know from your experience with Six Sigma, Sigma (the Greek letter σ) is a statistical term that measures *standard deviation*. In the context of management, it's used to measure defects in the outputs of a process and show how far the process deviates from perfection. (We'll get into the statistics in later chapters.)

A one-sigma process produces 691462.5 defects per million opportunities, which translates to a percentage of satisfactory outputs of only 30.854%. That's obviously really poor performance. If we have processes functioning at a three sigma level, this means we're producing 66807.2 errors per million opportu-

Sigma (σ) A term used in statistics to represent standard deviation, an indicator of the degree of variation in a set of measurements or a process. A one-sigma process produces 691462.5 defects per million opportunities—a percentage of satisfactory outputs of only 30.854%.

Standard deviation A measure of the spread of data points in relation to the mean. It's the most common measure of variation in a set of data.

Six Sigma A philosophy of managing that focuses on eliminating defects through practices that emphasize understanding, measuring, and improving processes. It's based on the statistical concept of six sigma, measuring a process at only 3.4 defects per million opportunities (DPMO).

Defect A measurable characteristic of the process or its output that is not within the acceptable customer limits, i.e., not conforming to specifications. The sigma level of a process is calculated in terms of defects per million opportunities (DPMO).

Capability Index	Defects per million opportunities	Percent of output defect free
6 sigma	3.4	99.99966%
5.5 sigma	32	99.9968%
5 sigma	230	99.97%
4.5 sigma	1,350	99.865%
4 sigma	6,210	99.4%
3.5 sigma	22,800	97.72%
3 sigma	66,800	93.3%
2.5 sigma	159,000	84.1%
2 sigma	308,000	69.2%
1.5 sigma	500,000	50%
1 sigma	690,000	31%
0.5 sigma	841,000	16%

Figure 1-1. DPMO at sigma levels

nities, delivering 93.319% satisfactory outputs. That's much better, but we're still wasting money and disappointing our customers.

Most organizations in the U.S. are operating at three to four sigma quality levels. That means they could be losing up to 25% of their total revenue due to processes that deliver too many defects—defects that take up time and effort to repair as well as make customers unhappy.

It's Only Words ....

Smart managers realize the impact of words. Be sensitive to the possibility that the word "defects" may bother employees. You may prefer instead to use the word "nonconformance." As D.H. Stamatis writes in the preface to *Six Sigma and Beyond: Foundations of Excellent Performance* (CRC Press, 2002):

"(We prefer the term nonconformance for legal reasons. The traditional verbiage has been defective.) A nonconformance is a deviation from the requirement."

Whether you use "defect" or "nonconformance" or any other word, what matters is that you're measuring things that are not right with your products or services—without blaming people or making them feel defensive.

A Goal—and a Process

Smart Managing   The concept of Six Sigma is to eliminate defects. Six sigma is the goal, but it's less important than the objective of pursuing continuing process improvement.

Sometimes the Six Sigma implementation team needs to set more realistic goals, depending on customer requirements and expectations and the complexity of the product or service. Smart managers know that the six sigma quality level is an idea; what's real is the focus on identifying defects and eliminating their root causes.

The central idea of Six Sigma management is that if you can measure the defects in a process, you can systematically figure out ways to eliminate them, to approach a quality level of zero defects.

The goal is to get the maximum return on your Six Sigma investment by spreading it throughout your company, continuing to train employees in the Six Sigma methodology and tools to lead process improvement teams, and sustaining the exponential gains you achieve by keeping it going.

But in addition to the expanding practice of the methodology and dollars redirected to the bottom line, there's another dimension to consider. Six Sigma doesn't exist in a vacuum; while its principles remain constant, there's an evolution of its message that can take companies in exciting new directions.

Design for Six Sigma

We're referring to the discipline known as *Design for Six Sigma* (DFSS)—an approach to designing or redesigning product and/or services to meet or exceed customer requirements and expectations.

Robert G. Cooper states in *Winning at New Products: Accelerating the Process from Idea to Launch* (Cambridge, MA: Perseus Books, 2001, 3rd edition) that only about 60% of new products launched are actually a success and that for every seven new product ideas, only four make it to development—and then only one succeeds. What's wrong with this picture?

The new product cycle is definitely not operating at a six sigma level. In fact, it's closer to the average four sigma quality level at which many companies operate today. Plus, even as manufacturing problems are corrected by deploying Six Sigma methods, newly developed products often are the source of new

> **Design for Six Sigma (DFSS)** A systematic methodology using tools, training, and measurements to enable the design of products, services, and processes that meet customer expectations at Six Sigma quality levels. DFSS optimizes your design process to achieve six sigma performance and integrates characteristics of Six Sigma at the outset of new product development with a disciplined set of tools.

problems. So, an organization practicing the methodology in various functional areas and attaining Six Sigma status may well be far below that level in developing new products or services.

Once you've mastered the essentials of Six Sigma, you may well be ready for the essentials of DFSS, to carry that improvement into the development and design of your new products. DFSS is based on the notion that when you design Six Sigma

> ### Prepare for the Elevator
>
> It's smart to have a 30-second explanation of DFSS, an "elevator" speech, to answer a question that people are likely to ask. Here's one proposed by Jim Parnella, Staff Statistician for Alcoa, Point Comfort, TX:
>
> Six Sigma is a disciplined, data-driven approach to process improvement aimed at the near-elimination of defects from every product, process, and transaction. The purpose of Six Sigma is to gain breakthrough knowledge on how to improve processes to do things *better, faster,* and at *lower cost.* It can be used to improve every facet of business, from production, to human resources, to order entry, to technical support. Six Sigma can be used for any activity that is concerned with cost, timeliness, and quality of results. Unlike previous quality improvement efforts, Six Sigma is designed to provide tangible business results, cost savings that are directly traceable to the bottom line.

quality right at the outset of new product development, it's probable that you'll sustain that gain as customers accept that product. By incorporating DFSS, you're virtually assured that the product or service you're launching will perform dependably in the marketplace, thus setting it up for very positive acceptance.

Like its parent Six Sigma initiative, DFSS uses a disciplined set of tools to bring high quality to launches.

It begins by conducting a gap analysis of your entire product development system. A gap analysis, as explained in Chapter 3, finds the gaps in your processes that are negatively affecting new product performance. It also addresses a highly significant factor, the voice of the customer (VOC). Every new product decision must be driven by the VOC; otherwise, what basis do you have for introducing it? By learning how to identify that voice and respond to it, you're in a far better position to deliver a new product or service that customers actually want!

Once the gap analysis is done and the VOC is identified, DFSS goes to work with its own version of the DMAIC (define, measure, analyze, improve, and control) of Six Sigma, a five-step process, known by the acronym PIDOV:

- Plan—enable the team to succeed with the project by mapping all vital steps
- Identify—hear the voice of the customer to select the best product concept
- Design—build a thorough knowledge base about the product and its processes
- Optimize—achieve a balance of quality, cost, and time to market
- Validate—demonstrate with data that the voice of the customer has been heard and that customer expectations have been satisfied

Some Six Sigma people equate DFSS with another five-step process—DMADV:

- Define—determine the project goals and the requirements of customers (external and internal)

- Measure—assess customer needs and specifications
- Analyze—examine process options to meet customer requirements
- Design—develop the process to meet the customer requirements
- Verify—check the design to ensure that it's meeting customer requirements

Others use only the IDOV steps listed above. Design for Six Sigma is relatively new, so we can naturally expect some inconsistencies and evolution of the models as companies and consultants apply them.

The success of this Six Sigma offshoot requires the active participation of management. You and upper management must monitor its progress regularly to keep it on course. DFSS can be a very useful tool to companies as they get comfortable with Six Sigma and look to grow its benefits in other areas.

Ultimately, DFSS is not that different from the Six Sigma work you're undertaking. In fact, it's a natural progression to continually—and relentlessly—root out defects and route hidden dollars to the bottom line.

Because of the similarities between Six Sigma and DFSS, people frequently talk about DFSS as the logical extension of Six Sigma at the manufacturing and service level, DMAIC. This may be true, but it's important to realize the initiatives are tremendously different. Here are the basic differences between the Six Sigma DMAIC and DFSS:

- DMAIC is more focused on reacting, on detecting and resolving problems, while DFSS tends to be more proactive, a means of preventing problems.
- DMAIC is for products or services that the organization offers currently; DFSS is for the design of new products or services and processes.
- DMAIC is based on manufacturing or transactional processes and DFSS is focused on marketing, R&D, and design.

- Dollar benefits obtained from DMAIC can be quantified rather quickly, while the benefits from DFSS are more difficult to quantify and tend to be much more long-term. It can take six to 12 months after the launch of the new product before you will obtain proper accounting on the impact of a DFSS initiative.
- DFSS involves greater cultural change than DMAIC, because for many organizations DFSS represents a huge change in roles. The DFSS team is cross-functional: it's key for the entire team to be involved in all aspects of the design process, from market research to product launch.

Design for Six Sigma Defined and Explained

DFSS is a business process focused on improving profitability. Properly applied, it generates the right product or service at the right time at the right cost. Through its use of product and team scorecards, it's a powerful program management technique.

DFSS is an enhancement to your new product development process, not a replacement for it. A documented, well-understood, and useful new product development process is fundamental to a successful DFSS program.

Your new product development process provides the roadmap to success. DFSS provides tools and teamwork to get the job done efficiently and effectively. By rigorously applying the tools of DFSS, you can be assured of predictable product quality.

Roots of DFSS

DFSS has its roots in systems engineering. In turn, much of the learning that underpins systems engineering evolved under the guidance of the Department of Defense and NASA. To control the lifecycle process, they developed a management approach that uses performance specifications, as opposed to volumes of product, subsystem, assembly, part, and process specifications.

In the systems engineering world, management of requirements (such as those aspects of the end product that must meet customer expectations) guides and drives the entire process.

Requirements at the senior or point-of-use level can then evolve through use of a variety of techniques generally described under the heading of *requirements flow-down*.

When statistical or quantitative methods are used to establish requirements between system performance and underlying inputs, the design process methodology tran-

> **Key Term**
>
> **Requirements flowdown** The process by which all high-level requirements are allocated to the various elements of a system, to make sure that some part of the process is meeting every requirement and no requirement is neglected.

sitions from a reactive, build-and-test mode to a predictive, balanced, and optimized progression.

DFSS provides a systematic integration of tools, methods, processes, and team members throughout product and process design. Initiatives vary dramatically from company to company, but typically start with a charter (linked to the organization's strategic plan), an assessment of customer needs, a functional analysis, an identification of critical-to-quality characteristics (CTQs), concept selection, a detailed design of products and processes, and control plans.

The beginning of the process centers on discovering customer wants and needs using tools such as Concept Engineering™ (Center for Quality of Management) and quality function deployment (QFD). From this "fuzzy" front end, requirements take shape. Customer issues, competitive advances, technology

> **Key Term**
>
> **CTQ** Critical-to-quality characteristics, the select few, measurable characteristics that are key to a specific part of the product, service, or process that must be in statistical control in order to guarantee customer satisfaction.

roadmaps, and disruptive influences commingle in a stew of initial uncertainty.

The Marketing Basics Around DFSS

Understanding the needs of the customer for a particular market segment is critical to success. We must get it right in this important first stage. All too often, however, this does not happen. Far too often, organizations do little more than review complaints and simply ask the customers what new features they would like to have added to the product. That's valuable, of course, but it's not going far enough.

Focus groups and interviews can also provide valuable information about the customer, but many times respondents offer feedback couched in terms of technical solutions. Customers offer technical solutions because they believe this is the best solution they're aware of. For example, they may want a laptop computer with a 40 GB disk drive, but what is their underlying need? Do they want faster boot-up time, storage space for pictures, audio, video? It's far better for the design team to understand the latent underlying need and then allow the technical arm of the design team to determine the best technical solution. In Chapter 3 we'll touch upon a technique called *contextual inquiry* that's valuable in helping us understand true, underlying customer needs.

Myths and Misconceptions About DFSS

One common misconception about DFSS is that it's a replacement for your current new product development process. If no formal process exists within your company, it could be used to guide the development process, but typically DFSS provides the tools, teamwork, and data to supplement the new product development process already in place in an organization.

Another misconception is that DFSS is just Six Sigma in design. The truth, simply put, is that DFSS is a complex methodology of systems engineering analysis that uses statistical methods.

Related beliefs are that DFSS is just Design for Manufacturability and Assembly (DFMA) and/or Design of

Experiments (DOE) and Robust Design concepts in engineering. (We'll get to those and other concepts and tools in Chapters 7 and 8.) Those beliefs are based on an overly simplified understanding of DFSS. It's actually a comprehensive process that involves DFMA issues and applies DOE and Robust Design among many methods.

Because of its use of statistical methods, people may believe that DFSS demands extensive statistical analysis and modeling of all requirements. This is untrue. DFSS calls for dealing with each engineering requirement optimally. Consequently, some requirements are analyzed statistically but some requirements are handled with traditional engineering methods.

Another misconception is that DFSS allows too much design margin, so that costs are higher, and/or increases development cycle times, so that market opportunities are missed. In fact, however, DFSS balances cost, cycle times and schedule, and quality.

Some people think of DFSS as being simply a collection of tools. This is a misunderstanding. Although DFSS uses some powerful tools, those tools alone will not ensure success, not unless those using them know how to apply them to specific engineering design opportunities.

Another misconception is that DFSS involves just the core product design team and has no impact on marketing, research, and manufacturing. Because of tools recently added to DFSS, this is no longer true. The most effective product development teams are cross-functional, with strong project management leadership and management support. Marketing, research, design, and advanced manufacturing engineering are typical representatives in a DFSS wave. The team works together to scope customer requirements, select design concepts, detail the product and process design, select suppliers, and ensure that supplier capability meets or exceeds customer-driven engineering needs.

One comment that we hear is that DFSS may apply to

many engineering disciplines, but not to all. However, since DFSS is not specific to any discipline, it applies to all. The analysis will differ according to the discipline, but most of the DFSS principles will apply.

Another misconception is that all management needs to do is "sign the check" and DFSS will happen overnight. Management must play an important role in leading the change effort. Activities such as linking the DFSS process with the company vision, establishing an executive change council to drive implementation, making successes visible, guiding implementation throughout the organization, and making DFSS integral to the company culture are all vital.

Start with a Firm Foundation

Before beginning DFSS in your organization, it may be wise to address any misconceptions about it, to make sure that everybody has a solid understanding and appropriate expectations.

Another misconception involves classroom training. Training in tools with no implementation plan does not result in cultural change. Far too many organizations develop or purchase extensive training initiatives, train employees in a classroom environment, and expect implementation to just happen. Classroom training that is not integral to implementation does not work. Another approach is just-in-time training. Team members learn about a tool as they need it; initial facilitation support is provided as they learn how to apply the tool and simultaneously work on the new product.

Manager's Checklist for Chapter 1

❑ Six Sigma is a philosophy of managing that focuses on eliminating defects by understanding, measuring, and improving processes. The methodology is based on measuring processes in terms of defects—most specifically the statistical concept of six sigma, which means only 3.4 defects per million opportunities. Six Sigma uses a five-step process—Define, Measure, Analyze, Improve, and Control (DMAIC).

❏ Design for Six Sigma (DFSS) is a systematic methodology using tools, training, and measurements to enable the design of products, services, and processes that meet customer expectations at Six Sigma quality levels. DFSS optimizes the design process to achieve six sigma performance and integrates characteristics of Six Sigma methodology in product development.

❏ Design for Six Sigma is relatively new, so there are differences in the models as companies and consultants apply them. Some use the following five-step process:
- Plan
- Identify
- Design
- Optimize
- Validate

Others use another five-step process:
- Define
- Measure
- Analyze
- Design
- Verify

❏ DFSS is surrounded by myths and misconceptions. It may be wise to address any of these in your organization before beginning DFSS, to make sure that everybody has a solid understanding and appropriate expectations.

Why Do Design for Six Sigma?

Now that you know a little about DFSS, you may be wondering if it's right for your organization.

The purpose of this chapter is to make the case for DFSS—or at least convince you that it's worth it to read the rest of this book.

Let's start with two basic questions:

- How does your organization develop new products and services?
- What is the ratio of product or service failures to product or service successes in your organization?

Why New Products and Services Fail

As mentioned in Chapter 1, it's estimated that only about 60% of new products launched in all industries are a success and that about 45% of resources allocated to developing and commercializing new products go into products that are killed or fail to provide adequate financial return (Robert G. Cooper, *Winning at New Products*).

The following reasons were cited as causes for the failure of new products by the percentage of companies indicated (Cooper, p. 25):

- inadequate market analysis: 24%
- product problems or defects: 16%
- lack of effective marketing effort: 14%
- higher costs than anticipated: 10%
- competitive strength or reaction: 9%
- poor timing of introduction: 8%
- technical or production problems: 6%

It's obvious that DFSS could help companies overcome many of the problems that cause new products to fail.

DFSS is a rigorous approach to designing products, services, and processes to ensure that the products and services meet customer expectations. It also enables the organization to reduce time, improve quality, and benefit financially.

The classical or traditional approach to designing products, services, and processes generally involves several functional departments working in *series*. This approach tends to lengthen the development process and increases the opportunities for defects at each step of the process. Communication among groups has little impact on the overall definition, because the process engineering is serial and drawing rework is the accepted norm. Each manufacturing challenge must then be quickly resolved with short-term fixes. At this point, root causes are either difficult to identify or expensive to fix and are therefore not pursued.

DFSS, on the other hand, is a *parallel* (concurrent) activity, with all relevant areas of the organization represented within a cross-functional team. There's a vast psychological difference between performing a task within a functional group and performing it as a cross-functional team member. When people from different functional groups and with different experiences and skills work together toward goals that will affect large areas, there's a synergy that maximizes what each individual brings to the project. Furthermore, all relevant knowledge and information is made available to the teams, so they can base their decisions on data rather than on judgment, as in the traditional approach. Product and/or service designs and manufacturing and/or transactional processes can therefore be developed together; as a result, products or services and processes can be made optimal relative to each other.

The advantages of DFSS are numerous:

- Provide a structure for managing development projects.
- Add value and improve customer satisfaction.
- Anticipate problems and avoid them.
- Minimize design changes.
- Reduce development cycle times.
- Reduce life cycle cost.
- Reduce manufacturing cycle times and time to market.
- Improve product quality, reliability, and durability.
- Improve communication among functions, particularly sales and marketing, product development, and manufacturing.
- Reduce costs of after-sale service and support.

These advantages can be summed up in the following four terms: customer satisfaction, quality, time, and money.

DFSS and the Customer

Conventional design processes tend to rely on assumptions about product features and services that will sell. DFSS goes to the logical extreme, to start with the essential question—What will customers buy? You'll recognize here a concept essential to Six Sigma—the voice of the customer (VOC).

DFSS identifies key customer needs before starting a design project and then prioritizes and translates these requirements into the design. These customer requirements (known variously as *critical-to-customer* or *critical-to-satisfaction* characteristics—*CTCs* or *CTSs*—or *critical-to-quality* characteristics—*CTQs*) are combined with cost factors (*critical to-cost* characteristics—

How Important Is VOC?

IBM was using Six Sigma in the early 1990s to improve product quality. But those quality improvement efforts didn't reveal a major problem: it wasn't building the right products.

IBM was reducing the defects in its networking equipment—but Cisco Systems Inc. was developing a new type of networking equipment, routers. IBM was improving its disk drives—but EMC Corp. was taking a new approach, redundant arrays of inexpensive disks (RAID). With those innovations, Cisco and EMC moved ahead of IBM in their markets; IBM has never recovered in either area.

CTCs) and time factors (*critical to schedule* characteristics—CTSs), and other quality factors in making design decisions. The team can then establish specific step targets for each component and for the process. (We'll discuss these and other *CTx's*—as we call them collectively—when we discuss metrics in Chapter 4.)

CTx's Factors that are considered critical in terms of the customer (CTCs) or some criterion, such as quality (CTQs), cost (CTCs), and schedule (CTSs).

DFSS and Quality

DFSS improves the quality of new products and services because it focuses on determining customer requirements, expectations, and priorities from the start. This is the first type of quality, from the perspective of the customer.

It also prioritizes other quality factors in design decisions, a second type of quality, from the perspec-

What Is "Good"?

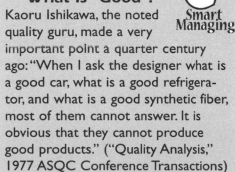

Kaoru Ishikawa, the noted quality guru, made a very important point a quarter century ago: "When I ask the designer what is a good car, what is a good refrigerator, and what is a good synthetic fiber, most of them cannot answer. It is obvious that they cannot produce good products." ("Quality Analysis," 1977 ASQC Conference Transactions)

Do you know what would make your products or services "good" from your customers' perspectives? If so, how do you know? If not, why not?

> ### Extending DFSS Beyond the Walls
>
> PACCAR Inc.—the company that manufactures Kenworth and Peterbilt trucks, among others—announced in January 2002 plans to use DFSS techniques in the design of its new products. In addition, PACCAR is involving the entire supply chain by requiring key suppliers selected for future product development to participate in PACCAR's DFSS training to ensure the quality of their designs. According to VP Helene Mawyer, "PACCAR is addressing the entire supply chain from the individual components provided by its suppliers to the final products and services delivered to its customers." Suppliers will participate on the PACCAR Six Sigma project teams and will be required to produce components of higher quality. PACCAR will favor higher-sigma suppliers, as their costs will be lower.

tive of the organization. The project team follows these basic steps:

- It defines requirements (customer, company, and regulatory).
- It works to find creative ways to meet those requirements.
- It anticipates things that could go wrong.
- It optimizes the function of the design in terms of costs and benefits.
- It verifies that the product or service meets the requirements.

If Six Sigma defines quality as conformance to specifications, then Design for Six Sigma must establish those specifications, within the organization and even beyond, extending the expectation of six sigma to suppliers. (We'll discuss this aspect of DFSS in Chapter 9.)

DFSS and Time

For many businesses, the old axiom, "Time is money," has become "Speed is life." Companies feel more and more pressure to develop and provide products and services with greater value at lower cost in less time. DFSS allows an organization to reduce time to market—once the organization acquires some experience in applying the principles and the tools. In almost any area of business, time to develop new products and services is a critical success factor. Generally, an organization that decreases its cycle time captures a greater share of the market.

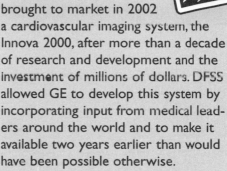

Time to Market

GE Medical Systems brought to market in 2002 a cardiovascular imaging system, the Innova 2000, after more than a decade of research and development and the investment of millions of dollars. DFSS allowed GE to develop this system by incorporating input from medical leaders around the world and to make it available two years earlier than would have been possible otherwise.

What is the financial value of getting this product on the market two years earlier? Only time will tell. But DFSS certainly gave GE Medical Systems a competitive advantage.

DFSS and the Bottom Line

Design for Six Sigma provides many tangible benefits to organizations. The approach results in long-term cost reductions, especially in the following areas:

- development and verification
- manufacturing and/or transactional processes
- service and support after the sale

When we say "long-term cost reductions," how much do we mean? It's estimated that companies performing at the current average quality level of four sigma lose 25% percent of their total revenue because of defects in processes and products.

Development and Verification

Reducing life cycle costs is a primary goal of DFSS. These costs may not be reduced, however, when first applying DFSS in the development process. While some costs will decline, others will rise because of the need to determine what the customers require or expect. But these initial costs will be recovered as the process is improved. The structured design development process focuses on getting products and services right as

Cost of Poor Quality

TOOLS When discussing sigma levels and defects per million opportunities (DPMO), it may be of use to refer to the following table that shows an estimate of the cost of poor quality (as a percentage of sales) at each level and in terms of DPMO:

Sigma	DPMO	Cost of Poor Quality
6	3.4	<10% of sales
5	230	10%-15% of sales
4	6,200	15%-20% of sales
3	67,000	20%-30% of sales
2	310,000	30%-40% of sales
1	700,000	>40% of sales

efficiently as possible. When there are established priorities and requirements for design and development activities, iterations and verifications are fewer, easier, and therefore less costly.

The conventional R&D approach starts from the perspective of developers and moves through designs and prototypes through iterations of building and testing. It later causes numerous design changes and wasteful rework and thus incurs losses in terms of the cost of poor quality. With DFSS, in contrast, design starts from the perspective of customers and designs are analyzed through modeling and simulation before prototypes are built and tested.

The later design errors are detected in manufacturing operations or process problems in transactional operations, the higher the cost—and the differences can be dramatic. It makes sense and saves dollars to detect problems at the earliest point and to prevent them if possible. That's the logic of Six Sigma: reducing variations is important at any point, but the further upstream the better.

Manufacturing and/or Transactional Processes

Processes—whether manufacturing or transactional—are considered in every DFSS project. That's only logical, of course.

Achieving the optimal design for a product or a service is the starting point; the project team must then work on the processes that deliver that product or service, to optimize their design as well.

This is where an organization can realize substantial savings in time and materials. By focusing on improving the design of products, services, and processes, DFSS can help reduce the time and material costs of poor quality—scrap, rework, repair, inspection, delays, customer complaints, returns, recalls, lost sales, and accounts ....

Service and Support After the Sale

When you design products, services, and processes from the perspective of your customers and focus on customer CTQs, the fewer problems you'll have with customer service and support.

The better the design, in terms of customer requirements, expectations, and priorities and in terms of quality, the easier it is to provide service and support—maintenance, repairs, troubleshooting, and so on.

Also, since DFSS begins with customers, employees throughout the organization are more focused on customers, thinking more from the perspective of customers. When employees are motivated in terms of the interests of their customers, it makes a big difference!

Even a Little Improvement at the Start ....

Figure 2-1 shows how DFSS in the planning stages can save in the operational stages. These rough estimates would amount to a savings of 15%.

Figure 2-1 shows that, although design typically represents the smallest actual cost element in products, it leverages the largest cost influence. Any incremental improvement in the design has a large direct impact on cost. For example, a 30% savings through design simplification would translate into over 21% cost savings overall, while the same 30% applied to labor or overhead would result in just 1.5% savings overall.

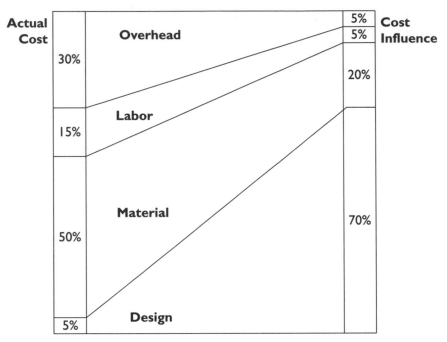

Figure 2-1. Impact of DFSS in product design
Source: *Six Sigma: The Breakthrough Management Strategy
Revolutionizing the World's Top Corporations*, by Mikel J. Harry and
Richard Schroeder (2000)

The main reason is that elemental improvement focuses on
optimizing a part or process, whereas DFSS may simplify or
even eliminate a part or a process. Any improvement in materials, labor, or overhead is unlikely to affect the other areas. In
contrast, a simplification in design will often result in a direct
reduction in material and labor cost and an indirect reduction in
the cost of overhead.

Competitive Advantages

It hardly seems necessary to stress the competitive advantages
of DFSS for the organization. Earlier in this chapter, we listed 10
general benefits of DFSS, benefits that can result in considerable competitive advantage.

Work in Both Areas

Six Sigma is hot and getting hotter, while the focus on design is relatively slow to get attention.

That's primarily because it's easier to quantify the benefits of Six Sigma, because it works with existing problems. It's easier to make the case for solving problems than it is to argue for the benefits of avoiding problems with better designs.

But good organizations use Six Sigma methods and tools to improve quality in both areas. After all, if you don't assign DFSS teams to improve the design process, how can you expect to have fewer problems for your Six Sigma teams later on—after you realize the problems that could have been detected and eliminated during testing?

Using DFSS, you can quantify these benefits to make the business case for pursuing DFSS projects. You don't need to "sell" DFSS: you can let the facts do that for you. We'll explain this vital step a little later in the book.

Intangible Benefits of DFSS

The focus in DFSS is on tangible benefits, advantages that can be quantified. But here's an interesting comment from Dennis Adsit, Senior Vice President of Rath & Strong, Inc. ("Six Sigma's Intangibles," *Leadership Report*, Spring 1999): "The real benefits are new ways of thinking and a culture of accountability that manifest when a company earnestly pursues Six Sigma."

He points out that employees and managers learn to think in terms of the customers, statistics, and cause-and-effect. And these ways of thinking and the strategies and tools develop a culture of accountability—

Accountability to customers to drive out variation and meet their specifications; accountability to shareholders to improve efficiency of internal processes; and accountability to employees to make the investments and remove roadblocks so efficiency and effectiveness improvements can be achieved and maintained.

What is the value of these new ways of thinking and this culture of accountability? You may not be able to quantify the value, but your organization will definitely be better because of these intangible benefits—which will add to your competitive advantages.

There are advantages for employees as well. When an organization is more committed to doing things right to better satisfy its customers and decisions are based on a common understanding of Six Sigma, employees tend to be happier— and they should benefit from the competitive advantages through higher pay.

More Than Just Tools

People often ask me if DFSS is really something different. They point out that most of the tools used in DFSS are not new and that companies are using many of these tools in their processes, different processes for developing new services and products without DFSS.

That's a good and valid point. But DFSS is more than just a collection of tools.

Essential in DFSS is the formalization of a structured and standardized development process that can be used throughout an organization. Whatever the functional area, it can apply the steps of the process and use the tools, according to its specific functions and needs. DFSS uses sophisticated statistical tools that most organizations have not been using in developing new products and services. And DFSS emphasizes training of all design teams, so everybody involved knows about the principles, methods, and tools, and so black belts and green belts are able to ensure appropriate leadership for cross-functional project teams.

High Expectations and Hard Reality

We've all heard about what Six Sigma can do for organizations. Some of the success stories have been well publicized. But why don't all organizations benefit significantly from the money and effort invested in DFSS?

All the talk about Six Sigma has created high expectations.

> ## Do It Right—or Not at All
>
> Thomas Pyzdek, in concluding his article, "In Defense of
> Six Sigma" (*Quality Digest*, March 2002), sums up the case
> for Six Sigma:
>
> When done properly, the net result of deploying Six Sigma is an
> organization that does a better job of serving owners and cus-
> tomers. Employees who adapt to the new culture are better paid
> and happier. The work environment is exciting and dynamic, and
> change becomes a way of life. Decisions are based on reason and
> rationality, rather than on mysterious back-room politics.
>
> However, when done half-heartedly, Six Sigma ... is a colossal
> waste of money and time. Either do it right, or don't do it at all.

But we must keep in mind the hard reality: it's a methodology,
not a strategy—and certainly not a panacea. DFSS can help
organizations design processes, products, and services to
reduce defects, to minimize variations from specifications. But it
may not necessarily translate into the results expected if it's not
an integral part of a general strategy. That's the reality that will
determine what benefits your organization can gain from DFSS.

It seems appropriate to conclude this presentation of the
reasons for using DSFF with a comment by Subir Chowdhury
(*Design for Six Sigma*):

Design for Six Sigma provides the means to accelerate
innovation, which is why GE, Caterpillar, Delphi
Automotive Systems, Dow Chemical, and others have
already entered the Design for Six Sigma race. Many others will follow just as they have in pursuing Six Sigma.
Those who excel in Design for Six Sigma will win; those
who don't will face a very perilous future.

In the next chapter, we'll outline the phases of DFSS. Then,
in Chapter 4, we'll discuss business metrics for DFSS. Chapters
5 and 6 focus on implementing DFSS and the human resources
that are vital to success. The following two chapters outline and
explain the basic tools used in DFSS. Chapter 9 will help you
sustain the initiative and continue to build on the advantages.

Finally, we'll conclude with a few case studies, to show how DFSS has worked.

Now that you know how DFSS is a logical and necessary part of Six Sigma and the reasons for investing in DFSS, we can move into the phases that give this approach its essential structure.

Manager's Checklist for Chapter 2

❑ About 45% of resources allocated to developing and commercializing new products go into products that are killed or fail to provide adequate financial return, for the following reasons:
- inadequate market analysis: 24%
- product problems or defects: 16%
- lack of effective marketing effort: 14%
- higher costs than anticipated: 10%
- competitive strength or reaction: 9%
- poor timing of introduction: 8%
- technical or production problems: 6%

❑ DFSS is a rigorous approach to designing products, services, and processes to ensure that the products and services meet customer expectations and enable the organization to reduce time, improve quality, and benefit financially. The advantages of DFSS are numerous:
- Provide a structure for managing development projects.
- Add value and improve customer satisfaction.
- Anticipate problems and avoid them.
- Minimize design changes.
- Reduce development cycle times.
- Reduce life cycle cost.
- Reduce manufacturing cycle times and time to market.
- Improve product quality, reliability, and durability.
- Improve communication among functions, particularly sales and marketing, product development, and manufacturing.
- Reduce costs of after-sale service and support.

❏ It could be argued that the real benefits of DFSS are new ways of thinking and a culture of accountability that come with a true and complete commitment to Six Sigma.

❏ DFSS works not just because of the tools but also because it requires a structured and standardized development process.

Core of Design for *Six Sigma*

As noted in Chapter 1, DFSS could be defined as "a rigorous approach to designing products, services, and/or processes to reduce delivery time, development cost, increase effectiveness, and better satisfy the customers." DFSS is not an established methodology. In fact, it could be argued that any design activity that leads to products or services or processes performing at a six sigma level should be considered part of DFSS.

Although we're using IDOV (Identify, Design, Optimize, and Verify) as the basis for our explanation of DFSS, what we say about the core of this approach applies in general to the other versions, including the following:

- DMADV—Define, Measure, Analyze, Design, and Verify
- DMADOV—Design, Measure, Analyze, Design, Optimize, and Verify
- DMCDOV—Define, Measure, Characterize, Design, Optimize, and Verify
- DCOV—Define, Characterize, Optimize, and Verify

- DCCDI—Define, Customer, Concept, Design, and Implement
- DMEDI—Define, Measure, Explore, Develop, and Implement
- DMADIC—Define, Measure, Analyze, Design, Implement, and Control
- RCI—Define and Develop Requirements, Define and Develop Concepts, and Define and Develop Improvements

Although these approaches to DFSS differ in some respects, they proceed through basically similar steps toward the same basic goals using common tools. They all fit the definition of DFSS as "a rigorous approach to designing products, services, and/or processes to reduce delivery time, development cost, increase effectiveness, and better satisfy the customers."

In terms of a basic procedure, it could be outlined as follows:

- The customer requirements are captured.
- The requirements are analyzed and prioritized.
- A design is developed.
- The requirements flow down from the system level to sub-systems, components, and processes.
- The capability of the product or service and process is tracked at each step and gaps between requirements and capabilities are highlighted and made actionable.
- A control plan is established.

Transfer function The basic equation of Design for Six Sigma, $Y = f(x)$ or $Y = f(x1 + x2 + x3 \ldots + x1x2 + x1x3 + \ldots)$. This equation defines the relationship between a dependent variable (Y) and independent variables (the X's). This is the structure of the model that helps us understand a process, used to represent relationships between the variables that are the causes and the dependent outputs of a process. The models could be regression equation, response surface fit, simulation model, finite element model, physics model, etc. Also known as an *engineering model*.

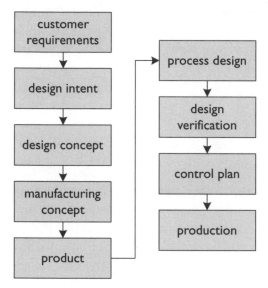

Figure 3-1. Generic design process

Depicted simply, DFSS does not differ greatly from the generic engineering process (Figure 3-1).

However, the value of DFSS lies in the details of the approach, the attitude (focus on six sigma), and the tools (statistical and nonstatistical).

The DFSS method has been represented as in Figure 3-2.

This is a *CTQ flowdown*—when a system (process and/or design) is diagrammed to identify the transfer functions (dependencies) between Ys and Xs at various levels of the system, such that the X's at one level are the Y's at a lower level and the Y's at one level are the X's at a higher level.

The DFSS approach varies, of course, according to whether the design is of a product or of a process. It may also vary according to the type of product. For example, in their book, *Design for Six Sigma in Technology and Product Development* (Prentice Hall PTR, 2003), Clyde M. Creveling, Jeffrey Lee Slutsky, and David Antis, Jr. distinguish between I^{2}DOV (Invent and Innovate, Develop, Optimize, and Verify) for developing *technology* and CDOV (Concept Development, Design

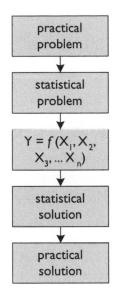

Figure 3-2. DFSS design process

Development, Optimization, and Verification of Capability) for designing *products*. Even within the IDOV approach (as within any other version of DFSS), there's a lot of flexibility and variations.

Changes

DFSS focuses on the design of products, services, and processes. But smart managers know that implementing DFSS or any other initiative successfully involves massive cultural change across the organization. DFSS will directly impact people in R&D, product design, advanced manufacturing engineering, manufacturing, marketing, distribution, and sales. All will be asked to make fundamental changes in their day-to-day roles in new product development.

As we all know, people generally do not want to change. We oppose change unless we recognize the necessity for it. Management plays an essential role in leading and managing the change effort within the organization. Communication is also essential, so that people throughout the organization know what is happening and why. We'll discuss the importance of management and communication in the implementation of DFSS in Chapter 5. But first we'll go through the core procedures. Some of the techniques and tools will be familiar to you through your experience with Six Sigma; some aspects, however, are specific to DFSS. (In Chapters 7 and 8, we'll get into the tools, some of which will be familiar to you from Six Sigma.)

The IDOV Method

Since, as we've pointed out, any design activity that leads to products or services or processes performing at a six sigma level could be considered part of DFSS, the IDOV method sometimes begins with a Plan or Prerequisites phase. For that reason, to present IDOV more completely, we're including the Plan/Prerequisites phase. If IDOV is used without the Plan phase, the steps are included in the Design phase.

Here are the basic purposes of the phases in a complete IDOV approach:

- **Plan/Prerequisites:** to set up the team to succeed with the project by mapping all of the vital steps
- **Identify:** to select the best product or service concept based on the voice of the customer (VOC)
- **Design:** to build a thorough base of knowledge about the product or service and its process
- **Optimize:** to achieve a balance of quality, cost, and time to market
- **Verify/Validate:** to demonstrate that the product or process satisfies the requirements

However a DFSS approach may be structured into phases or stages, it's important for management oversight and control to set up a mechanism known variously as a *phase-gate review*, a *stage-gate review*, a *project review*, a *phase review*, a *project tollgate review*, or a *project milestone review*. Through this mechanism, a management team reviews and assesses the project at the end of each phase according to the plan set forth in the project charter and well-defined criteria. The

Key Term

Project review A management review or decision gate set up at any key point in the project—usually at the end of a stage or a phase—to allow a management team to review progress, assess the project, and determine whether or not it should continue. Also known as a *stage-gate review*, a *phase-gate review*, a *phase review*, a *project tollgate review*, or a *project milestone review*.

managers review timelines and check key progress deliverables. They then decide whether or not the project is successful at that point and worth further expenditure of resources.

Now, let's examine each of these phases in detail. Our examination will not be very specific, because the IDOV approach is just one of several, as we've noted. DFSS adapts to the nature and needs of the organizations and differences among products and services and processes. Even if we accept the assertion by Geoff Tennant (mentioned in Chapter 1) that there's little difference (at least in theory) between a product and service, there are many significant differences in terms of applying DFSS techniques and tools. We'll outline steps and techniques in this chapter and present many of the tools mentioned here a little later, in Chapters 7 and 8.

P—Plan/Prerequisites Phase

The purpose of the Plan/Prerequisites phase is to set up the team to succeed with the project by mapping all of the vital steps. It entails selecting the project, providing managers to support the project, choosing people to form the team (a black belt, green belts, and others), conducting training, establishing a project charter and objectives, setting metrics and a goal, and establishing a timeline.

Procedure

Select the project. It should be a highly visible development project. The selection may be made based on any of the following: customer comments, customer surveys, input from within the organization (e.g. from R&D, Sales, Marketing), benchmarking, and multi-generation planning (MGP).

Initiate the project. Every project should have a well-defined implementation plan with responsibilities, timetables, milestones, and deliverables. The team schedules phase-gate reviews to provide for a rigorous examination of progress on the project at the end of each phase of the DFSS process.

Select the champion or sponsor. The champion is critical to any Six Sigma project. The champion should be an upper-level manager who is responsible for new product development and can handle the responsibilities of a champion part-time. This person must have the authority to ensure that the project team is successful. The concept of "champion" comes to us from the Middle Ages, when a champion was a person who fought for a cause. In Six Sigma, a champion is an advocate who fights for a project against barriers—functional, financial, personal, or other—so that the project team members can do their work. The champion:

- Establishes project goals.
- Chooses the black belts and the green belts.
- Provides direction.
- Allocates resources.
- Breaks through barriers.
- Holds team members accountable for the project goals.
- Asks for the results.
- Ensures that the project is on track.
- Is devoted to doing whatever it takes to make the project successful.
- Interfaces with executive managers.

In brief, the role of the champion is to support the DFSS process. A strong champion is vital to the success of any DFSS project. (We'll discuss the champion again in Chapter 5.)

Select the black belt. As for any Six Sigma project, a black belt appointed to lead a DFSS project should have a strong desire to

Champion A senior-level manager who promotes the Six Sigma methodology throughout the company and especially in specific functional groups. The champion understands the discipline and tools of Six Sigma, selects projects, establishes measurable objectives, serves as coach and mentor, removes barriers, and dedicates resources in support of black belts. A champion "owns" the process—monitoring projects and measuring the savings realized.

do things differently and better, to be change agent. He or she should have outstanding people skills, communication skills, and facilitation skills. In addition, for a DFSS project, the black belt should be skilled in product development. The responsibilities of the black belt are as follows:

Credible Champion

It's essential to select a champion who is responsible for product design. The director of human resources, the quality VP, or the head of strategic planning, for example, will just not have the necessary credibility with the DFSS team or others throughout the organization to make the change a long-term reality.

- Commit full-time to the project.
- Achieve the project goals.
- Facilitate the use of DFSS tools.
- Coach and mentor team members.
- Break through barriers.
- Translate between the team and others in the organization.
- Keep the project scorecards.
- Coordinate all project team activities.

(We'll discuss the responsibilities of the black belt in greater detail in Chapter 5.)

Select green belts and team members. Choose open-minded, highly skilled people from all areas affected by the DFSS project, such as

Check—Don't Just Check Off!

Smart managers do not simply sign off on a project and ignore what's happening. Just as with any product, service, or process in the organization, a DFSS project must be judged rigorously, according to high standards. Rubber stamping is contrary to Six Sigma.

marketing, design, manufacturing, quality assurance, and vendor development. The team should represent all of the key functions that contribute to developing and testing the design

Black belt A full-time change agent trained in the methodology to solve product and process defects project by project with financially beneficial results. A black belt does Six Sigma analyses and works with others to put improvements in place.

and then working with the product, service, or process. Some team members will work on the project from beginning to end; others will contribute only during certain phases.

The members must have functional expertise and knowledge relevant and sufficient to the project. Each member has specific duties and responsibilities for making the project successful. Team members must be willing to try something new. They must understand that their roles will change, that the DFSS initiative will require things of them that are very different from traditional roles. Some members will experience discomfort with this new approach. They need to understand this is normal and that, with practice, the new tasks will become easier. (We'll discuss the responsibilities of the green belts in Chapter 5.)

Conduct "just-in-time" training. Because team members are under pressure to meet deadlines, make sure that their training is linked to real work. As the tools of DFSS are presented, team members should be applying them to the project.

Define the implementation schedule.

Define the attendance matrix. This is a summary of the people who should attend each of the training sessions. For instance, the market requirements folks will need to attend the training sessions on VOC activities but not the sessions on tools such as FMEA or control planning.

No Sheep Dips! Do not immerse people in DFSS principles and tools. That's more indoctrination than training—and it's not an effective way to make changes in the organization. Provide training that is relevant and practical when team members are ready to apply what they learn.

Establish the project charter. As you know, this is a key step in Six Sigma methodology. The basic purpose of a project charter is to formalize the DFSS initiative, to capture the vision of the project, to convey a feeling of enthusiasm, to set direction for the project team, and to define the parameters of the project. It should include the following elements:

- Name the project. Give it a title that describes it appropriately and succinctly.
- Identify the project leader and the mentor or master black belt who will serve as resource for the project leader.
- Define the scope. The scope outlines what the project is and what it is not.
- Define the starting point and the end point.
- Identify the deliverables.
- Set the goals.
- Ascertain the resources.
- Recognize and assess the risks.
- Set the start date.
- Set the anticipated end date.
- Create the business case.
- Plan for organizational buy-in.

Establish the project objectives. This step consists essentially of three parts:

- *Define the metrics.* The metrics provide a measurable, quantitative scale for assessing performance. They answer the question, How do we assess our progress?
- *Collect baseline data.* The baseline defines a starting point, based on the competition, similar products or services, etc. It answers the question, Where are we beginning?
- *Set the improvement goal.* The goal defines an improvement target. It answers the question, "What is our goal?" This is based on entitlement, which is the theoretical maximum performance possible.

Defining the Project

Smart Managing The team must determine and agree upon objectives and bounds for the project. It may help to think in terms of SMART objectives—specific, measurable, achievable, relevant, and timed. A team that takes on a project with objectives that do not meet all five criteria will probably have difficulty.

Setting project metrics is crucial—which is why Chapter 4 is devoted to them. They should represent the voice of the customer and internal metrics selected by the organization. They should be simple and vital to the design and they should be in terms that all team members understand. They should be connected to key business metrics. (It may be unnecessary to point out here that there's no single metric that meets all the requirements for a specific situation.)

Establish the timeline. This should include major milestones.

Develop the strategic plan. The project team elaborates the plan put in place earlier by executive management.

Review lessons learned. Team members should plan to share and document what they learn throughout the project. A good time to do this is when the project passes through a phase-gate. The first project review is most important in this respect, since it sets a precedent for sharing information and communicating.

Identify channels for process capability data. How will you know what results you're achieving? Process capability data is essential in allowing members of the team to contrast engineering requirements with process capability. (If the necessary process capability data does not exist, the team must flag this gap and make it actionable.) (We'll discuss process capability in Chapter 8.)

Conduct a measurement system analysis (MSA). This step is key to getting good process data.

Map the process. The purpose of drawing up a process map is to show how the process flows, to list and categorize all the key process variables (KPVs) and to begin understanding how key process input variables (KPIVs) generate key process output variables (KPOVs).

> **Measurement System Analysis**
> This is an experimental, mathematical method for determining to what extent variation within the measurement process contributes to overall process variability. In an MSA, there are five parameters to investigate: bias, linearity, stability, repeatability, and reproducibility. (We'll discuss MSA in Chapters 4 and 8.)

Plan for communicating project information.
Getting the word out to appropriate people in the organization, especially stakeholders, is important. The plan should specify who will communicate what to whom, why, how, and when.

> **Key process variable (KPV)** A process component that is involved in a cause-and-effect relationship of sufficient magnitude. There are two types: *key process input variable (KPIV) (X's)* and *key process output variable (KPOV) (Y's)*.

Conduct the Plan/Prerequisites phase-gate project review.

I—Identify Phase

The purpose of the Identify phase is to select the best product or service concept based on voice of the customer. The focus here is on defining the requirements of the product or service. The team identifies the customer, the critical-to-quality specifications (CTQs), the technical requirements, and the quality targets.

Procedure

Define the customer. The team may use a SIPOC (supplier-input-process-output-customer) map for the product or service to help identify and even prioritize customers. The team considers internal customers as well as external. At this point, the team may use a prioritization matrix to distinguish among the customers.

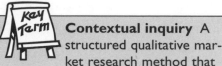

Contextual inquiry A structured qualitative market research method that uses a combination of techniques to discover customer needs through observing and interviewing people in the context of using the product or service.

Identify and understand the customer requirements. Gathering VOC (voice of customer) is essential to DFSS. There are various means of capturing customer information; some capture expressed needs and others are used to discover latent needs. The means of gathering VOC include the following:

- reviews of customer complaints
- surveys (including preference surveys to define the relative importance of customer preferences)
- focus groups
- one-on-one interviews
- contextual inquiry
- customer specifications
- field reports
- conjoint analysis
- interactive prototyping

To organize the customer inputs, the team might use a tool such as an affinity diagram or a VOC table, a tool for recording information about customer needs that allows the team to capture the context of those needs to better understand explicit and implicit customer requirements. To categorize customer requirements in terms of levels of customer satisfaction, the Kano model is useful. (This tool is

TOOLS

Conjoint Analysis This methodology for exploring subjective customer perspectives allows team members to avoid direct questioning about a feature ("What do you think of this feature?") through asking customers what they would be willing to pay for that feature. Conjoint analysis simulates real-life decisions in which customers consider different cost-benefit alternatives.

Interactive prototyping The process of building working models of a product or a service, trying them out, and modifying them according to input from users. Interactive prototype enable much richer testing of a design, but it's also the most expensive and often time-consuming way to get input from potential customers.

explained in Chapter 7.)

Quality function deployment (QFD) uses a house of quality method to identify factors that are critical to customer satisfaction and factors that are critical to quality, connected through complex $Y = f(X)$ transfer functions. The house is used to rank the importance of features that affect meeting the performance specifications.

Be Sensitive and Be Smart

Avoid becoming too zealous in seeking the voice of the customer. Long surveys, detailed instruments, and requests for personal information can easily try the patience of all but the most helpful customers. Think of the experience from your customers' perspective. With all VOC tools, remember: choose and use judiciously.

(We'll discuss quality function deployment and enter into the house of quality in Chapter 7.)

Prioritize customer requirements. The team analyzes customer feedback and marketing data. It then quantifies and

Affinity Diagramming

After the team has gathered information on customer requirements and expectations, it needs to organize the information. If it needs to consolidate disparate items from interview notes, survey results, market research, and so forth into a selection of essential statements, affinity diagramming can be a useful tool. Team members transcribe onto cards brief statements of customer requirements and expectations. They then organize these cards into logical groupings of related needs. This makes it easier to identify similarities and redundancies and ensure that key needs are represented. Also known as the *KJ method*, after its inventor, Kawakita Jiro.

Voice of the Customer Table

TOOLS This tool is not only useful in recording information about customer needs in context, but it also serves as a preliminary exercise before the team builds a QFD house of quality.

For each customer statement, the team enters demographic information and information about the use of the target product or service. The information is categorized to provide a context for analyzing the statements. The statements are then translated into requirements. (The VOC table is presented in greater detail in Chapter 7.)

ranks benefits to the customers, using such tools as rank ordering, sensitivity analysis, tradeoff analysis, and analytic hierarchy process to weigh the relative importance of each requirement. (Chapter 7 will present the analytic hierarchy process.) The team may also use FMEA, which can provide an excellent basis for classifying CTQs and other critical variables and to help the team direct resources toward the most promising opportunities. The team may supplement its use of FMEA at this point with quality function deployment to help plan preventive actions.

Establish other requirements—organizational, regulatory, environmental, and so forth.

Identify the CTQs and technical requirements, performance targets, and specification limits. The team translates customer and other requirements into critical-to-quality features (CTQs), using quality function deployment (QFD).

Prioritize the CTQs. The team uses QFD and Failure Modes and Effects Analysis (FMEA) to prioritize critical-to-quality features.

Document the CTQs in formal specifications. The team identifies technical requirements, performance targets, and specification limits. It sets a target and a range of acceptability for each CTQ, using benchmarking and competitive analysis. It may also decide to establish performance baselines, if designing a replacement or redesigning, in order to understand the current design well enough to ensure that it will achieve significant results by focusing on what matters to the customers, not the current design.

Establish CTQ metrics. The team establishes ways to measure to what extent the product or service design meets the specifications. We'll discuss metrics in Chapter 4, including the importance for product designs of analyzing measurement system capability.

The Danger of Benchmarking

Since DFSS is for designing products, services, and processes, benchmarking is usually less useful than for Six Sigma projects. It's worth studying best practices for the Plan and Identify phases, but it may not help in actually developing a design. In fact, sometimes comparisons—even with the best—can hinder creativity.

Create the scorecards. Throughout the project, the team uses the scorecards to record design requirements, capture information, estimate performance, track results, and make any gaps obvious and actionable. In the Identify phase, the team lists the CTQs and the metrics.

Select the design concept. The team takes the information from the first phase of QFD and addresses potential design concepts for the various subsystems within the design. Typically, many subsystems and components can be reused or highly leveraged from previous generations of the design. For subsystems or components that will not be leveraged, the Pugh concept selection process is very useful. The team takes the concept(s) provided for the new product or service in the Plan phase and develops the concept(s) into a working paper design, generating concepts that address all the key requirements. DFSS teams also frequently conduct a preliminary FMEA for each design concept at this point. If designing a product, the team could also conduct a design for a manufacture and assembly (DFMA) test on each alternative concept.

Move from a focus on CTQs to a focus on critical-to-process metrics (CTPs). By the end of this stage, the team will have a

Pugh Selection Matrix

This matrix, developed by Stuart Pugh in the early 1980s, provides a structured way to choose among alternatives—and it encourages the team to generate better ways to meet the criteria. The Pugh matrix structures comparisons of alternatives against selection criteria. The team uses the tool iteratively to arrive at an optimum choice. Also known as Pugh's method, controlled convergence matrix, decision-matrix method, or simply the selection matrix. (We'll discuss this further in Chapter 7.)

set of design concepts and with a set of CTPs that will constrain the formal and technical design.

Analyze the influence of the CTQs on the technical requirements. The team can use QFD I (house of quality) to translate customer CTQs into technical requirements (CTQs for engineering).

Develop innovative alternatives to satisfy the functional requirements. The team may use any of the various tools for stimulating innovative thinking, such as brainstorming. One methodology being promoted as useful for identifying design alternatives is TRIZ. Although TRIZ can be a great tool for thinking out of the box and so a valuable tool for advanced development and R&D groups, it's not much in use by DFSS teams, because the potential solutions generated may take years to prove out.

Think Different!

Smart Managing Managers who want results are smart to encourage project team members to indulge in divergent thinking. Consider the comment about process redesign by Peter S. Pande, Robert P. Neuman, and Roland R. Cavanagh in *The Six Sigma Way* (McGraw-Hill, 2000, p. 315):

Envisioning, designing, and then operationalizing a new work process can be an almost schizophrenic effort. The team needs to display different "personalities" as it tries to break down accepted norms and fears, identify new workflows and procedures, and then construct a new way of doing work.

Perform risk analysis. The team uses FMEA to reduce the possibilities that things could go wrong.

Consider means of error proofing. The team could use any of the Design for X tools listed in Chapter 7, as appropriate— Design for Manufacture and Assembly, Design for Reliability, Design for Testability/Testing, Design for Cost, Design for Serviceability, and so on. It could also apply poka yoke, the first step in error-proofing, which we'll discuss in Chapter 8.

Perform an engineering analysis and select materials. If it's a product that the team is designing, it can use engineering analysis such as simulation and then computer programs for material selection.

(One software package worth noting is from Granta Design. It's based on the methodology for materials selection developed by Michael F. Ashby, author of *Materials Selection in Mechanical Design* [Second Edition, Woburn, MA: Butterworth-Heinemann, 1999]. The methodology provides a systematic and quantitative approach to materials selection. The software allows a team to develop formal selection models that provide a case history for a selection issue.)

Two Types of Quality

It's important to distinguish between two types of quality— customer quality and production and/or delivery quality. The former consists of providing the features in products or services that will satisfy the customers and the latter is eliminating or minimizing the effect of problems in products or services that will dissatisfy the customers.

The team addresses customer quality primarily through VOC techniques and QFD and addresses production/delivery quality through tools such as FMEA and/or variants such as design failure modes and effects analysis (DFMEA) (for components and subsystems), process failure modes and effects analysis (PFMEA) (for manufacturing and assembly processes), and service failure modes and effects analysis (SFMEA) (for service functions).

Do preliminary work toward planning procurement and manufacturing.

Select equipment based on needed capability. This is especially important for products with long lead times.

Formulate the concept design and predict the sigma level of quality. The team uses Pugh's method to evaluate design concepts and refine and strengthen them, hybridizing as appropriate, to select a best solution concept for optimizing.

Conduct the Identify phase-gate project review.

D—Design Phase

The purpose of the Design phase is to build a thorough base of knowledge about the product or service and its processes. The team translates the customer CTQs into functional requirements and alternative concepts or solutions; through a selection process, the team evaluates the alternatives and reduces the list of solutions to one, the best-fit concept.

Procedure

Formulate concept design. In evaluating design alternatives, the team uses the Pugh concept selection technique on the first pass. This will allows the team to select or improve upon the best alternatives. The next mode of evaluation is based on FMEA. Here teams will evaluate a selected design concept for potential failure modes so that they can be addressed early in the design effort.

Identify part and process CTQs. For each technical requirement, the team identifies critical-to-quality design parameters (CTQs) and their influence on the technical requirements (transfer functions), using analysis, Design of Experiments (DOE, explained in Chapter 8), simulation, and/or modeling— representations of the relationships ($Y = f(X)$) between customer requirements (Y's) and design elements (X's).

Populate the DFSS scorecard. At this point, the team records CTQs on the project scorecard. Scorecards typically contain CTQs, specification, process capability data, process capability calculation, and flags (for any processes for which process capability may be inadequate).

> **Modeling** Representation of relationships between independent input variables (X's) and dependent output variables (Y's), as variations on the basic formula, $Y = f(X)$. In other words, the output of a process is a function of the inputs. You can be sure of the outputs only if you can control the inputs. Models can be based on empirical methods, simulation, or physical fundamentals.

Quantify transfer functions. The team develops and refines transfer functions through means such as the following:

- Benchmarking historical transfer functions.
- Performing analytical simulations.
- Conducting designed experiments or tests.

The team then applies transfer functions to develop the general layout and to approximate overall performance. It records the transfer functions on the project scorecard.

Establish target values and tolerances. The team does this with parameter and tolerance design, such as *empirical tolerance design* and *analytical tolerance design,* to create a robust design. Tolerance analysis is also a valuable tool: it enables quantitative estimation of the effects of variation on requirements in the early phases. Three common models of tolerance analysis in design are *worst case tolerance analysis, statistical tolerance analysis,* and *root-sum-square analysis.* For tolerance prediction and analysis, the team can

> **Tolerance design** The science of predicting the effects of component tolerances and environmental change on a system and optimizing the design of that system for quality, cost, and time to market. Two usual types are *empirical tolerance design* and *analytical tolerance design.*

Root-sum-square analysis A statistical method for establishing system capability based on the capability of the parts of that system.

Assess process capability The team should calculate process capability indices Cp, Cpk, and Cr. (These are discussed in Chapter 8.)

Cp A capability index that tells how well a system can meet two-sided specification limits, assuming that the average is centered on the target value.

Cpk A capability index that tells how well a system can meet two-sided specification limits.

Cr A capability ratio that is the reciprocal of Cp. It's calculated with the estimated sigma.

Ppk A performance index that tells how well a system is meeting the specifications. It's calculated with actual sigma (sigma of the individuals).

Pp A performance index that summarizes the performance of a process in terms of meeting upper and lower specification limits.

Pr A performance ratio summarizes the spread of the process in comparison with the spread of the upper and lower specification limits.

also use Monte Carlo simulation methods. (Chapter 8 will discuss tolerance design and analysis, including Monte Carlo.)

Assess process performance. The team should calculate process performance indices Pp, Ppk, and Pr. (These are discussed in Chapter 8.)

Do a gap analysis. The team tries to find any gaps in the processes that are negatively affecting the performance of the new design. To depict gaps, a spider diagram is practical.

Identify, assess, address, and manage risks. The team uses FMEA to better understand the risks and compensate for them.

Assess Design for X, depending upon the product or service. The tests could be Design for Manufacture, Design for Assembly, DFMA—Design for Manufacture and Assembly, Design for Reliability, Design for Testability/Testing, Design for Cost, Design for Serviceability/Service, Design for Quality,

> ## Spider Diagram
> This "graphic report card" represents the performance of
> a number of aspects on one chart and shows the gaps
> between the current performance and the target. The team places the
> aspects on a circle and then evaluates the status of each in relation to
> the target, assigning each a rating, with 10 being the ideal, the target.
> Used alone, the spider diagram graphically depicts where and how
> much work remains to be done. If the team uses it with an *interrela-
> tionship digraph*, each aspect gets a score, so the team can prioritize
> areas to focus on improving. Also known as a *gap analysis tool* or a
> *radar chart.*

Design for Fabrication, Design for Disassembly, Design for
Diagnosis, Design for Inspection, Design for International,
Design for Green or for Environment, Design for Environment,
Safety, and Health ....

Update the scorecards.

Conduct the Design phase-gate project review.

O—Optimize Phase

The purpose of the Optimize phase is to achieve a balance of
quality, cost, and time to market. The team uses advanced statistical tools and modeling to predict quality level, reliability, and
performance. It uses process capability information and a statistical approach to tolerancing to develop detailed design elements and optimize design and performance.

Procedure

Identify potential failures. Perform FMEA or Anticipatory
Failure Determination (AFD). Both tools apply to both the
design of the product and the design of the process. Use reliability data to make predictions of field failure rates. The team
can also use pilot and small-scale implementations to test and
evaluate performance. At this stage, testing should be to finalize
the design, not to try out design ideas.

Take corrective action to mitigate or prevent those failures.

Anticipatory Failure Determination (AFD) This failure analysis method, like FMEA, is used to identify and mitigate failures—but in reverse. Rather than looking for a cause of a failure mode, the project team views the given failure as an intended consequence and searches for ways to produce the failure reliably. (AFD will be presented in detail in Chapter 8.)

Develop a robust design. The focus of the design process is to create a design that is robust, that can perform acceptably despite variations in design parameters, operating parameters, and processes. The team works to make the processes capable of meeting the design requirements, especially with critical design parameters and CTQs. It uses Design of Experiments (DOE) or Taguchi Methods to optimize parameter values and reduce variation. Optimization studies are performed to minimize the sensitivity of performance to CTQ design features and identify the processes most in need of improved capability.

Apply response surface methodology (RSM). Critical in optimizing process or product performance, RSM is usually applied following a set of designed experiments intended to screen out the unimportant factors. The primary purpose of RSM is to find the optimum settings for the factors that influence the response.

Apply evolutionary operations (EVOP), if appropriate.

Robust Relatively insensitive or impervious, in terms of outputs, to natural, unavoidable variations in inputs, processes, components, and materials, so the product or process performs as closely as possible to the target specifications.

Evolutionary operations (EVOP) A continuous improvement process for optimizing the operating conditions of a process. EVOP consists of systematically making small changes in the levels of the process variables being investigated, changes small enough to minimize the risk of serious disturbances in yield, quality, or critical product characteristics, yet large enough to reveal potential improvements in performance.

> ### Response Surface Methodology (RSM)
> This statistical technique uses response surfaces to analyze
> quantitative data from experiments to determine and simul-
> taneously solve multivariant equations. (A response surface is a surface
> that represents predicted responses to variations in factors.
> Depending on the number of factors, the surface can have any number
> of dimensions.) RSM allows the project team to predict the results of
> experiments without performing them.
>
>   Response surface methods can be used to answer a number of dif-
> ferent questions:
> 1. How do a set of variables affect a particular response over a spec-
>   ified region?
> 2. What settings of the variables will result in a product or process
>   that meets specifications?
> 3. What settings of the variables will yield a maximum (or minimum)
>   response and what is the local geography of the response sur-
>   face(s) near these maximal (minimal) values?

Update the CTQ selection. What CTQs have emerged at the subsystem or process level?

Update capability and MSA data.

Update the scorecards.

Conduct the Optimize phase-gate project review.

V—Verify/Validate Phase

The purpose of the Verify/Validate phase is to demonstrate that the product or service satisfies the voice of the customer, to ensure that the design will meet the customer CTQs. This phase consists of testing, verifying, and validating the design, assessing performance and reliability. The team tests prototypes and the design goes through iterations as necessary.

Procedure
Validate product or service and processes. This step may include testing prototypes.

Demonstrate the process capability.

Verify tolerances.

Evaluate reliability.

Conduct an MSA. The team checks again to determine to what extent variation within the measurement process contributes to overall process variability.

> **Statistical Process Control (SPC)** The application of statistical methods and tools to analyze data and monitor process capability and performance. Tools commonly used in SPC include the following:
> - Flow charts
> - Run charts
> - Pareto charts
> - Cause-and-effect diagrams
> - Frequency histograms
> - Control charts
> - Process capability studies
> - Acceptance sampling plans
> - Scatter diagrams

Implement Statistical Process Control (SPC).

Define and implement the control plan. Once the design has been proven to meet the specifications of the established requirements, the team takes action to stabilize the design. It sets up a control plan, so the process owners can monitor and maintain the process.

Update and validate the scorecards.

Conduct the **Validate/Verify phase-gate project review.**

The Basics by Any Name

The DFSS method—whether the PIDOV approach outlined here or variants—extends the power and discipline of Six Sigma to the beginning, where it makes the most difference in terms of time and money.

So, now you know the basics of DFSS, through the structure of the PIDOV approach. You should be able to adapt easily to other versions—DMADV, DMADOV, DCCDI, DMEDI, DMADIC, RCI, and so forth.

Each organization is unique and processes may vary greatly. Those responsible for DFSS projects will need to fine-tune their approach over time to make it best fit their organization. In chapter 5 you'll find some suggestions for implementation.

Manager's Checklist for Chapter 3

❏ DFSS is a rigorous approach to designing products, services, and/or processes to reduce delivery time, development cost, increase effectiveness, and better satisfy the customers. It is not an established methodology. Any design activity that leads to products or services or processes performing at a six sigma level should be considered part of DFSS.

❏ The various approaches to DFSS proceed through basically similar phases toward the same basic goals using common tools, although they differ in some respects. The approach outlined in this chapter consists of the following phases:
  • Plan/Prerequisites: to set up the team to succeed with the project by mapping all of the vital steps.
  • Identify: to select the best product or service concept based on the voice of the customer.
  • Design: to build a thorough base of knowledge about the product or service and its process.
  • Optimize: to achieve a balance of quality, cost, and time to market.
  • Verify/Validate: to demonstrate that the product or process satisfies the voice of the customer.

Design for Six Sigma Metrics

In God we trust; all others must bring data.
—W. Edwards Deming

If you're familiar with Six Sigma, you're familiar with the need for metrics. Without the right metrics, you can't really know how much progress you're making toward your goals. Metrics constitute the scorecard for your Six Sigma or DFSS projects. If you can measure your processes, you can understand them. If you can understand them, you can design them for superior performance. That means lower costs, higher quality, and greater customer acceptance.

In the area of metrics, there's a big difference between Six Sigma and Design for Six Sigma. Six Sigma focuses on one or two critical-to-quality (CTQ) metrics, examines processes, and works to improve the CTQ performance by about 1 process sigma. DFSS, in contrast, focuses on every CTQ that matters to any customer for a particular product or service and works to develop a new product or service that achieves a performance around 4.5 sigma or higher.

Business metric A unit of measurement that provides a way to objectively quantify a process. Any measurement that helps managers understand and improve their processes might be a business metric, such as the following:
- number of design verification tests passed the first time
- number of products completed per hour
- percent defective from a process
- hours required to provide a service
- months to design a product or service
- engineering change orders after production tooling kickoff
- mean time between failures (MTBF)

You'll recall that in Chapter 3, in discussing the project charter, we mentioned that an effective objective has three components:

- metrics
- baseline
- goal

With the metrics that it sets, the project team provides a measurable, quantitative scale for assessing performance on the project scorecards. This is one of the most crucial elements of the project charter.

The best way to set metrics for any DFSS project is to start with customer needs. The purpose of any metric should be to answer this basic question: How do you know the product, service, or process is achieving the established goals?

General Guidelines for Metrics

Before discussing metrics in more detail, we should establish several basic points:

- Metrics should be simple and straightforward and meaningful. Team members should be able to explain them to others.
- Metrics should create a common language among diverse team members.
- Metrics should be relatively easy to apply. They should not complicate operations and create excessive overhead.

- Metrics should call for information that can be collected accurately and completely.

When drafting metrics for a project, the team should consider how the metrics are connected and related to key business metrics. There's usually not a single metric that meets all the requirements of a particular situation.

What Should You Measure?

In designing a product or a service, the project team identifies certain factors as being critical. What's critical depends, of course, on the product or service being designed, the other products and services, the functional unit, and the structure and strategies of the organization.

What Matters for Your Customers?

The fundamental metrics are for the characteristics that matter most to the customers, external or internal—the critical-to-customer characteristics that constitute the first definition of quality.

These CTQs (critical to quality characteristics, as described briefly in Chapter 2) are the key measurable characteristics of a

---

Smart Managing

Know What the Customer Wants— and How Much

It's important to know how much something in a product or a service matters to your customers—and remember that it may change in importance. A *want* (basic need) is something the customer would like, but is usually not even verbalized by the customer since it's fundamental to the product or service. An *expectation* (spoken need) is something the customer received previously or elsewhere or knows exists; when asked about product features, the customer would express a *need*. A *delight* is something that exceeds the customer's needs or expectations, eliciting comments like "Wow! I have to have this!"

Over time, customer wants may become needs and even expectations, expectations may become needs, and delights may become expectations. Products or services that attract and keep customers now will not likely be enough for long.

product, service, or process that must meet certain performance standards or specification limits in order to satisfy the customers. We also call these expectations *requirements*, because
they're essential: they align design efforts with the customers.

CTQs must usually be translated from qualitative customer
statements into quantitative, measurable business specifications
using tools such as quality function deployment (QFD). The
project team sets metrics such as the following, defined in direct
relationship to the customer requirements:

- quality of the product, service, or process
- life cycle of the product, service, or process
- price vs. performance for specific market niches

Then, the project team should set internal metrics, to measure aspects such as these:

- critical-to-design characteristics
- critical-to-function parameters
- cost of the product or service and the resources to develop it
- critical-to-marketing characteristics
- time: critical to schedule, cycle time, throughput time,
  delivery time
- critical to business operations
- critical to organizational strategy, in alignment with the
  overall needs of the business
- compliance with government and other regulations

Metrics may be prioritized as critical to quality or primary
and non-critical or secondary. Each critical metric is tracked on
DFSS scorecards. Non-critical metrics are important and the
design must meet specifications, but they're not typically
tracked on a scorecard.

In selecting metrics for a project, the team should consider
balancing the scorecards. Many Six Sigma professionals advocate using balanced scorecards in selecting metrics, to ensure
that the project meets a wide range of needs. This approach

includes metrics that are financial, of course, but also metrics in other areas, such as internal processes and employee development. Typical metrics in the latter areas might include the following:

Internal Processes
- rolled throughput yield
- cycle time
- rework (hours and materials) and scrap
- quality of suppliers

Employee Development
- quality of training
- use of DFSS tools
- effectiveness of teamwork and meetings
- lessons learned
- adherence to project schedule
- number of projects completed
- savings (by project and total)

Whatever metrics the team selects, it sets step targets for each component and for the process, connecting metrics to every phase of the DFSS project.

Standards

For every metric, the team should set a standard. The standard

CAUTION!

Don't Measure Everything!
It's easy to measure: what's hard is to decide what to measure.

Software programs have made statistical analysis accessible even to novices, providing formulas and doing calculations both simple and complex. That's why it's increasingly important for DFSS project teams to keep their goals in mind when deciding on metrics. When establishing a metric, you need to know why you're measuring it, why it's important, and what's causing the results. Don't measure everything just because you can. Select metrics carefully. More is not necessarily better.

serves as the target, the criterion by which measurements are evaluated.

The basic general unit of measurement in six sigma is, of course, sigma—standard deviation, the measure of variation in a process. As you may recall, we defined standard deviation in Chapter 1 as a measure of the spread of data points in relation to the mean. We should be more specific here: it's a measure of the spread within a set of data, calculated as the square root of the average squared deviation of the data from the mean.

DPMO Definitions

The use of calculations of defects per million opportunities (DPMO) seems very objective and precise. But that's true only if the project team provides accurate definitions of the key terms, "defects" and "opportunities."

What is to be considered a *defect*? It's any instance in which the product or service fails to meet customer requirements or other specifications. So the team must determine unacceptable variations and describe each type of defect in terms that are unambiguous. Definitions could include photos or samples.

> **Key Term**
>
> **Defects per million opportunities (DPMO)** A measure of quality used in Six Sigma initiatives calculated by dividing the number of defects in a process by the number of opportunities, expressed as one million. The measure is often used to estimate the *sigma rating* of a process.
>
> **Defect** Any instance in which the product or service fails to meet customer requirements or other specifications.
>
> **Opportunity** Any situation in a process that presents a reasonable possibility of causing a defect.

What is to be considered an *opportunity*? It's any situation in a process that presents a reasonable possibility of causing a defect. The team must describe the various possibilities for defects. Opportunities are events or characteristics that might be incorrect.

> **⚠️ CAUTION!**
>
> **Prevent Denominator Management**
> When the project team chooses opportunity metrics poorly, the result can be what Thomas Pyzdek calls (*The Six Sigma Project Planner*) "denominator management"—manipulation of the measurement system. A denominator should represent the process that's being measured, not an earlier process or subprocess. If you have evidence that earlier opportunities are being included to inflate the denominator, you should bring it to the attention of the project champion. Six Sigma depends on honest measurements.

Here's an example. A magazine editor receives comments from readers about not being able to find a central repository of information regarding DFSS. The publisher decides to launch a quarterly publication on DFSS. One useful metric would be the number of new subscriptions per week.

If you establish metrics for incomplete shipments, for example, you should describe what constitutes "incomplete." Does it matter how many items are missing? Do you account for the relative importance of the items to the customer? If so, how? The problem of an incomplete shipment is worse if the customer refuses delivery, but how do you measure that effect? How do you establish a metric that doesn't require any of the employees to make judgments when they track the data?

Figure 4-1 shows a simple way for the project team to establish definitions of "defect" and "opportunity" to be used in calculating DPMO figures for the receptionists in a company call center.

How do you establish appropriate, accurate metrics? You tap the experience of the employees who are closest to the processes. You hold meetings to discuss your attempts at establishing metrics and you encourage everyone to find fault with them. Then, finally, as you use your metrics, encourage one and all to report any questions or problems with them.

Problems with Metrics Based on Defects

It's easy to get so caught up in measuring that you focus too much on quantifying defects and forget about also quantifying

CTQ	Defect (Definition)	Opportunity (Definition)
responsiveness to call	hold time of 60 seconds or more	call
protocol (hello, identification, goodbye)	omission or error	three per call
transfer of call	call transferred to wrong person	call

Figure 4-1. Establishing definitions for defects and opportunities

the effects. And that can lead to problems.

Here's an example. If you're setting metrics for your secretaries, you might include a measurement of typos (defects) in terms of 1000 characters (opportunities). So you determine that George averages 5 typos, Sarah averages 7, and Pat averages 8. The metrics show that George is the most accurate—if you quantify defects only. But what about the effects on your customers? George generally has more problems with names, while Sarah and Pat check names carefully. Since customers are usually more bothered by mistakes with their names than mistakes with other words, George causes more dissatisfaction than Sarah or Pat. That's one of the problems with being too focused on counting defects alone. So, if you decide to work on improving the design of this process, you would want to consider ways to reduce or even eliminate typos—but particularly with names.

Problems with Metrics Using Averages

Six Sigma allows you to measure variation in a process, to calculate standard deviations from the mean, for a more accurate picture of the process. Compare this with the usual way of representing a series of figures, which is by finding the average—an approach that can fail to reveal big problems.

Here's an example. You're working in shipping; your project is to design a distribution system that will enable the truck drivers to achieve at least 95% on-time deliveries. For your three

It's Variations, Not Averages!

Smart Managing   A smart manager always remembers, when working on designing a product or a service, that it's about variations from a standard, not about averages. A customer does not experience the average. He or she experiences individual variations.

As Jack Welch, former CEO of GE and staunch advocate of Six Sigma, put it in the GE 1998 annual report:

"We have tended to use all our energy and Six Sigma science to 'move the mean' .... The problem is, as has been said, 'the mean never happens' .... The customer only feels the variance that we have not yet removed."

drivers this month, you calculate averages of 15.3 minutes late, 24.7 minutes late, and 6.3 minutes late. So Driver 3 has the best average. But the averages don't show everything. In fact, they may allow some defects to counterbalance other defects. Here, the averages don't show that Driver 3 is often as late as Drivers 1 and 2, but occasionally arrives 20 to 30 minutes early. That helps improve her average—but it inconveniences the customer who expects deliveries on time—no sooner, no later. The averages also can hide extremes. The averages here don't show that Driver 1 has several times been late by 45 minutes, while Driver 2 has been late more often but never by more than 20 minutes.

In your DFSS projects, you can measure variations in a process and then focus on the variations that most affect your key metrics.

Exercise care in determining what is to be measured. Metrics should be based on what you need to measure to improve the process, rather than what fits the current measurement system. Scrutinize all metrics in terms of their value for understanding a process.

Question Everything

When creating metrics, the project team must ask questions—new questions—and search for new results. If you keep asking the same questions, you'll probably not come up with designs that are new or significantly different.

When the project team begins setting business metrics and asking questions, it should begin with the fundamentals:

- Why do we measure this?
- Why do we measure it in this way?
- What does this measurement mean?
- Why is this measurement important?

The team should ask questions, challenge answers, put assumptions to the test, and confront conventions. DFSS is basically zero-based thinking. The team should enlist the help of people who are known for their critical thinking skills, whether they're familiar with the processes or not, and encourage them to question and to challenge. That approach might be unusual in your company, but for DFSS it's the best way to start.

Whether you manage a small administrative staff or a large manufacturing division, by asking questions, examining the fundamentals, and establishing appropriate metrics, you're taking the right first step toward success with DFSS.

Leadership by Example

Establishing metrics requires dedication, focus, and logic. It also requires leadership. As manager, you must serve as a model of critical thinking and courage to challenge the status quo and underlying assumptions. You must ask yourself and people in your division and even throughout the organization why all of you do the things you do. When you challenge, when you ask new questions and start measuring the answers, you demonstrate leadership that inspires and encourages others to go above and beyond the status quo. By asking new questions, you

> **Making Metrics Work**
>
> When designing a product or a service, avoid measuring just to measure. Ask about the function of each metric and link it to your key criteria. Remember: if you don't ask the right questions, you won't get the right answers.

can develop metrics that will help you design to better meet the expectations of your customers and your business criteria.

SMART Metrics

As mentioned in Chapter 3, the DFSS project must set metrics that are **S**pecific, **M**easurable, **A**chievable, **R**elevant, and **T**imed (SMART):

- **S**pecific: targeted to the area being measured.
- **M**easurable: data can be collected that is accurate and complete.
- **A**chievable: possible for the team to realize.
- **R**elevant: important in terms of the specifications.
- **T**imed: providing data when it's needed.

At the risk of creating an acronym that isn't a word in English, we would also add "**A**ctionable: easy to understand and capable of showing where to take action." After all, if you create a metric that provides information but you can't do anything to improve the design or the process, are you making any progress?

Measurement Reliability and Validity

After the team establishes the product metrics, it should ensure that the means of measuring are going to produce data that is both *reliable* and *valid*. Information is *reliable* essentially if the same information is obtained from more than one trusted source. It does not guarantee that the characteristic being measured is the one intended. For that we have the concept of validity. Information is *valid* if it covers an area well enough to represent it accurately.

If the design is of a product, rather than a service, many of the met-

> **Key Term**
>
> **Reliability** The accuracy and consistency of a measurement and the consistency and dependability of a measuring instrument. In other words, if the measurement is repeated under the same conditions and the results are the same, it's reliable. Reliability does not guarantee that the characteristic being measured is the one intended.

rics will involve measurements of physical properties such as length, width, thickness, weight, shape, color, etc. To evaluate the reliability and validity of

> **Measurement system analysis (MSA)** The evaluation of measurement systems in order to detect and quantify errors in measurement.

dimensional measurement systems, such as gauges, the project team should do *a measurement systems analysis* (MSA).

The purpose of an MSA, conducted on all measurement devices, is to detect and quantify errors. It generally involves the following factors:

- **repeatability:** The degree of variation among repeated measurements, the ability of an instrument to reproduce a reading with certain accuracy.
- **reproducibility:** The degree of variation in the averages among appraisers repeatedly measuring the same characteristic of a single part.
- **stability:** The degree of variation in measurements when a known, constant input (a single characteristic) is measured over an extended time span.
- **linearity:** The difference in the bias values or repeatability across the expected operating range of the measuring instrument, consistency.
- **bias:** The difference between the observed average of measurements and the reference value. It's essentially an offset from "zero" (a drift), which necessitates adding a consistent "bias factor" to all measurements. Bias is often called "accuracy," the difference between the observed value and the true or accepted reference value.
- **discrimination:** The ability to distinguish differences, which requires enough increments for differences to be measured. If in doubt, apply the Rule of Ten—to have 10 possible values between limits is ideal, to have only five possible values is marginally useful, and to have four or fewer possible values does not allow for adequate discrimination.

Financial Linkage of Metrics and Results

There are two main concepts governing metrics. The first is *knowledge*: your metrics provide knowledge about your processes, which helps you develop better metrics. The second concept is *alignment*: your metrics must align with your strategic goals for performance.

When implementing metrics, it's critical to link them to overall performance. If your metrics don't align with your performance, then they can't tell you anything you really need to know.

Here's a quick example. A retail company promises in its "principles of doing business" to ship all items quickly and to train its sales and service employees to know its products, to be friendly, and to take care of customers. Any DFSS project to develop better service processes should align its metrics with these principles. The company promises quick shipping, so the team would track turnaround time and the timeliness of deliveries from its suppliers, but not overtime expenses. The company encourages employees to take care of customers, so the team would measure customer satisfaction, but not contact time, since that metric would not be in alignment with the performance goal of complete customer care.

Your metrics should link to your performance goals. Otherwise, you won't be getting the knowledge that you need about your processes—or you'll be working on areas that won't matter to your customers or could even disappoint, frustrate, or anger them. It's a simple point, but worth repeating: if your metrics don't align with your performance, then they can't possibly tell you anything you really need to know.

Guidelines for Metrics

Here are the basic steps in setting metrics:

Start with your customers. What's important to them?

Establish key, consistent metrics. What metrics do you need to measure what's important?

Determine baselines. What is the current state of your processes?

Benchmark processes. Who's doing the same or similar things better than you?

Set goals. Easier goals can mean quick successes; more ambitious goals can help sustain your DFSS initiative.

Here are some steps to help you select your metrics for the most useful results. These guidelines are simple, internal things to help the project team set metrics and get the information necessary to work through the phases of DFSS.

Involve the leaders. Since they set company strategy, they need to be involved in how the metrics are linked to achieving it. Any DFSS initiative will require a commitment of human and other resources from the top.

Represent your metrics visually. Prominently display them in charts, graphs, and diagrams, to show your employees what you're trying to do and how they are involved in delivering information and correcting the processes.

Metrics must respond quickly. Your measurement systems must provide feedback promptly, so you can identify problems in the design and/or processes and correct them as soon as possible.

Metrics must be simple. They must clearly communicate the information you need and be easy to use. If they require a lot of explanation and definition, then you make it more difficult to collect data and translate that data into actions.

Metrics should drive only important activities. Assess the most important factors to measure—and then make sure that what you examine will result in information that's relevant.

Limit the number of metrics. Generally, you should implement no more than 10 metrics at a given time, so you get feedback fast and don't get bogged down in measurements.

Adjust quickly. Once you have feedback, you and your team should make corrective adjustments as soon as possible.

Baselines

After you've determined the metrics that will provide you with the most important information about your processes, you use them to establish baselines. A baseline indicates the current status of your performance. In DFSS, quality function deployment (QFD) often replaces baseline measurements.

> **Key Term**
>
> **Baseline** The status of one or more key metrics at present, a standard for comparisons, a reference for measuring progress in improving a process. The baseline is contrasted with the *entitlement,* the theoretical maximum performance. The *goal* is what part of the entitlement the project is seeking to achieve.

In a way, baselining is similar to the thorough physical examination that you would undergo before beginning an exercise regimen. Just as your doctor would check out basic indicators of health, your baseline activity should measure key input variables, key process variables, and key output variables.

The focus of Six Sigma lies in a simple three-part formula: $Y = f(X)$. It represents the basic truth of a process: Output (Y) is a function of Input (X). This is just a mathematical way to state that variables or changes in inputs and the process will determine outputs.

The activity not only provides baselines, of course, but it also serves as a good test of your metrics. As you apply your metrics to establish baselines, you may find problems with some of them: maybe you need to modify metrics, drop metrics, and/or add metrics. Sometimes metrics that make sense on the drawing board just don't work as well when we put them to use.

Benchmarking

Benchmarking is a simple concept, but many managers may not understand how to do it. There are basically three types:

- **Internal**—Internal benchmarking determines the best business practices within your own organization. This is just a starting point—unless your current practices are best in class. The primary objective is to identify and define your current standards and to share them throughout the organization.
- **Competitive**—Competitive benchmarking includes research into the products, services, and processes of your direct competitors and/or the best-in-class competitors, in order to identify and describe them. The objective is to get information that will allow you to compare your products, services, and processes with what your competitors (direct or best in class) are offering.
- **Functional**—Functional benchmarking is identifying and examining products, services, and processes of organizations that do not compete with your organization, at least not directly. The objective is to learn from the activities of organizations considered to be the best in class in some function—manufacturing, management, customer service, human resources, finance, engineering, and so forth.

> **Benchmarking**
>
> Benchmarking has been defined as "the practice of being humble enough to admit that someone else is better at something and being wise enough to try to learn how to match and even surpass them at it."
>
> *Smart Managing*

Whether internal, competitive, or functional, benchmarking consists of the following six steps:

1. Define the product, service, or process identified as a benchmark.
2. Form a team to conduct the benchmarking.
3. Identify benchmarking resources.
4. Collect and analyze information.
5. Plan a course of action to improve the design of your product, service, or process.

6. Follow the plan!

Traditionally, the focus of benchmarking has been for an organization to assess itself against competitors in its industry. But that means living in the past, in the belief that matching or surpassing current competitors ensured success in the future. And it meant that organizations could feel secure if they offered a product or a service that was unique in some way. That approach would make the benchmarking activity of DFSS easier.

However, organizations should also take a functional approach. Managers should benchmark for each of the organization's operations against organizations that excel in that specific operation.

This approach can motivate and inspire an organization to appoint DFSS project teams for areas beyond its products and services.

When you've established your baselines, you understand the current state of your processes, you know where you are. Benchmarking allows you to figure out where you want to go with your processes. Through benchmarking, you can establish priorities and targets for designing a product, service, or process and identify ways to do so. As that great philosopher, Yogi Berra, once observed, "If you don't know where you are going, you will wind up somewhere else."

At this point, you know what you want to benchmark and you've got your metrics. Now what?

The next step is generally to identify benchmarks—internal or external—for your target processes. Since most Six Sigma initiatives use benchmarks outside the company and since that's more complicated than using internal benchmarks, external benchmarking will be our focus here.

How do you identify benchmarks? You find organizations that have target processes that perform better than yours in some way. You may know that through competitive intelligence, through media reports, and the Web, where articles that would have gone unnoticed in local publications or data that would have been buried in a report are now out there for you to access.

Next, you collect data on the target processes. How you do this depends on the processes, the benchmarks identified, and the sources of information. Use your creativity and investigative instincts and skills. You may be able to get information from public domain sources, through the library or the Web. Another approach is to purchase a competitor's product and do a *product teardown*, recording such metrics as product complexity and approximate cost. Some companies provide information in white papers, technical journals, conference presentations, panel discussions, and so forth, or in materials for vendors and customers or advertisements. You may need to develop questions for a survey to be conducted by mail, telephone, fax, or e-mail. You may decide to take the most direct approach, to contact companies and arrange site visits. You could also enter into a benchmarking partnership, in which each partner would gain information about the others in exchange for sharing information on its own processes. Another possibility is to work with a competitive intelligence firm.

> **Keep It Legal and Ethical** ⚠️ CAUTION!
>
> Benchmarking can be risky business. To minimize the likelihood of misunderstandings, ethical slips, and legal problems, you should follow the Benchmarking Code of Conduct scripted by the International Benchmarking Clearinghouse, a service of the American Productivity & Quality Center (www.apqc.org).

Once you've completed your benchmarking studies, you should have data for each of your key metrics for the targeted processes. Then, you're ready for the next step.

Gap Analysis

You've used your key metrics to establish baselines for designing your target product, service, or process. You've gathered benchmark data to show what you can expect from your design. Now, you compare. In technical terms, you do a *gap*

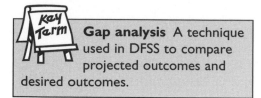

Gap analysis A technique used in DFSS to compare projected outcomes and desired outcomes.

analysis, to compare the outcomes you're projecting and the outcomes set as your goals.

Your gap analysis enables you to make changes in your design. It may also guide you to set additional metrics.

Some Statistics

Setting business metrics depends on a concept basic to Six Sigma—sigma. Anybody familiar with Six Sigma knows that sigma is a term used in statistics to represent standard deviation, an indicator of the degree of variation in a set of measurements or a process. So, assuming that you know at least the basics of Six Sigma, we can very briefly review variation and standard deviation. If you're experienced and comfortable with Six Sigma statistics, feel free to skip over this section!

Variation

Variation is defined as "any quantifiable difference between individual measurements." Any process improvement should reduce variation, so that we can more consistently meet the product or service requirements. But in order to reduce it, we must be able to measure it.

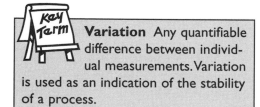

Variation Any quantifiable difference between individual measurements. Variation is used as an indication of the stability of a process.

There are several ways to measure variation, each with advantages and disadvantages.

We can use the *mean,* but that may not work very well, as we mentioned earlier in this chapter. Using one figure to represent a series of measurements may not reveal variations that could be significant. In our example, the driver with the best average for deliveries was late as often as the other two, but the average didn't show that variation because the driver also showed up early on occasion, which was also a problem. The driver with the best average delivery has been very late several times, much later than the other two drivers.

Mean Average (more specifically called the *arithmetic mean*), the sum of a series of values divided by the number of values.

Median Midpoint in a series of values.

Mode Value that occurs most often in a series of values.

We can use the *median* (the midpoint in a range of data). However, the median does not show if a process is allowing extreme variations on both sides of the specification limits. To use a very simple example, Process A and Process B both produce for a specific metric that measured median values of 6—which is just perfect for this metric. But, if we consider the measurements that produced this median of 6 for both processes, we find 1, 6, 7, 11, and 5 for Process A and 4, 6, 7, 5, and 8 for Process B. So, Process A is varying much more than Process B—but we wouldn't know it from the median.

We can also calculate the *mode* (the value that occurs most often). But, depending on the number and the precision of the measurements, the mode might not be of much value.

Based on these three measurements, what do we know about the variations in our two widget assembly lines? How do they compare? Which statistical concept best represents the variation in each line?

Fortunately, there are two more statistical concepts that we can use to better understand and control variation: *range* and *standard deviation*.

Range is easy to calculate: it's simply the spread, the difference between the highest value and the lowest value.

But range is a rough measure, because it uses only maximum and minimum values. That's why

Range Difference between the highest value and the lowest value in a series, the spread between the maximum and the minimum.

we use standard deviation, which is more accurate than range for calculating and representing process variation.

Standard deviation measures variation of values from the mean, using the following formula:

sigma = square root of epsilon (x − x bar) squared divided by n − I

where σ = sum of, X = observed values, X bar = arithmetic mean, and n = number of observations

That formula may seem complicated, but it's simple to understand if we break it down into steps:

$$\sigma = \sqrt{\frac{\Sigma\,(x - \bar{x})^2}{n - I}}$$

1. Find the average of the process values.
2. Subtract the average from each value.
3. Square the difference for each value (to eliminate any negative numbers from the equation).
4. Add all of these squared deviation values.
5. Divide the sum of squared deviations by the total number of values.
6. Take the square root of the result of that division.

If we plot enough values on a control chart, we'll likely find that the distribution of values forms some variant of a bell-shaped curve. This curve can assume various shapes. However, in a *normal* curve, statisticians have determined that about 68.2% of the values will be within 1 standard deviation of the mean, about 95.5% will be within 2 standard deviations, and 99.7% will be within 3 standard deviations.

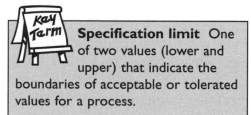

Specification limit One of two values (lower and upper) that indicate the boundaries of acceptable or tolerated values for a process.

Your goal with your DFSS project is to reduce the variation in the product or service and the processes. So you first need to determine how much variation is acceptable to your customer and for other requirements. Then, you use those values to set your *lower specification limit* (LSL) and your *upper specification limit* (USL)—the upper and lower boundaries within which the system must operate. (See Figure 4-2.)

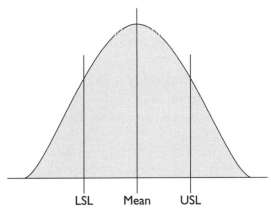

LSL   Mean   USL

Figure 4-2. Bell curve showing mean, lower specification limit and upper specification limit

Process Capability

So, how does this discussion of variation, standard deviation, and curves relate to DFSS? The goal of Six Sigma is to reduce the standard deviation of your process variation to the point that six standard deviations (six sigma) can fit within your specification limits.

> **Process capability** A statistical measure of inherent variation for a given event in a stable process,. the ability of a system to perform within its specification limits.
>
> **Process width** Spread of values +/- 3 sigma from the mean. Also known as *normal variation*.

The *process capability* is defined as a statistical measure of inherent variation for a given event in a stable process. In English, that means the ability of a system to perform within its specification limits. We defined three capability indices in Chapter 3. Now, let's focus on one of them, Cp.

The capability index Cp of a process is usually expressed as *process width* (the difference between USL and LSL) divided by six times the standard deviation (six sigma) of the process:

$$\frac{Cp = USL - LSL}{6\sigma}$$

The higher your Cp, the less variation in your process. (Capability can also be expressed with other indices: Cpk, Cr, and Cpm.)

The second process capability index, Cpk, splits the process capability of Cp into two values.

Cpk = the lesser of these two calculations:

$$\frac{USL - mean}{3\sigma} \quad or \quad \frac{mean - LSL}{3\sigma}$$

Another pair of limits should be plotted for any process—the *lower control limit* (LCL) and the *upper control limit* (LCL). These values mark the minimum and maximum inherent limits of the process, based on data collected from the process. If the control limits are within the specification limits or align with them, then the process is considered *capable* of meeting the specifications. If either or both of the control limits are outside the specification limits, then the process is considered *incapable* of meeting the specifications.

> **Key Term**
>
> **Control limit** One of two values (lower and upper) that indicate the inherent limits of a process in statistical process control (SPC). On a control chart, two horizontal lines are drawn to mark the upper control limit (UCL) and the lower control limit (LCL). The sample means and the ranges from a series of measurements must be within these limits. If so, the process is behaving normally and is "under control." If any point lies outside either limit, it indicates control.

Six Sigma Shift

The Six Sigma measure of process capability assumes that the process average may shift over the long term, despite all efforts to control it. Shift is a complex subject in Six Sigma. In simple terms, the shift is the degradation from the

The Shift: Past and Present

The calculation of 1.5 sigma for the shift between short-term capability and long-term performance comes from Motorola. The company determined, through years of experience, that every process drifts over time. What it called the *long-term dynamic mean variation* typically runs between 1.4 and 1.6.

However, in many circles, the shift is controversial. Some experts have argued against using this generic figure, citing research that shows that a 1.5 sigma shift cannot be generalized.

short-term capability to the long-term performance when all possible time-related causes of process variation have been considered.

("Short term" is the process capability at its best, without any time-related variation. The sigma value of every process, by convention, is the best short-term value. "Long term" is the process capability at its worst, with every possible time-related variation included.)

Conventionally the shift is calculated at 1.5 sigma, an empirical figure now considered standard—a default value to use until you obtain actual process data. So, process capability is generally reported in short-term sigma—without the presence of special cause variation. Then, to account for the process shift over time, long-term performance is determined by subtracting 1.5 sigma from the short-term calculation. Thus, if a process is operating at 6 sigma, you would compute the yield not as 2 parts per billion, according to a normal distribution table, but rather as 3.4 parts per million, which is 4.5 sigma—6 sigma less the 1.5 sigma shift.

Concepts and Calculations

As a manager, you may not need to crunch numbers using the formulas given in this chapter. What's important is that you understand the basic concepts of Six Sigma measurements and better appreciate the importance of establishing metrics to track variation so you can improve processes. You may not be able to perform all of these calculations and others used in DFSS.

That's why there's statistical software. You may not completely understand these concepts. That's why training is essential to any Six Sigma initiative.

Other Important Factors

Finally, any DFSS project team should keep in mind that the CTx approach to metrics will not ensure that the design of a product or a service takes into account all of the factors that are important.

Avoid Bad Metrics
When developing metrics, beware of the following:
- Metrics for which you cannot collect accurate or complete data.
- Metrics that are complex and difficult to explain to others.
- Metrics that complicate operations and create excessive overhead.
- Metrics that cause employees to act not in the best interests of the business, just to "make their numbers."

The team may want to consider, for example, employee morale, ergonomics, and the reaction of parties in other areas of the organization or in the community. Are there other factors that are important to the success of the project? If so, how can the team accommodate these factors in its design?

Conclusion

You should establish a checklist for metrics, with questions appropriate to the project and your specific situation. It should include the following general questions:

- What are the key metrics for this process?
- Are these metrics valid?
- Are these metrics reliable?
- Does everyone involved understand these metrics?
- Do we have adequate and accurate data?
- What is the baseline for each metric?
- What is the goal for each metric?

Be Sensitive

Set metrics to reveal changes of an appropriate magnitude, so you can monitor any significant variations in the process. What's significant? That depends on your baselines and your goals. It's important that your metrics capture changes in enough detail to enable you to take action to improve the design.

Now that you've got your metrics, we'll discuss the people who will be involved in the DFSS project and then discuss how to make the project a success.

Manager's Checklist for Chapter 4

❑ Measurement is crucial to the success of your DFSS initiative. Your metrics apply statistical tools to the results of your designs.

❑ Metrics must be clear and simple and must yield information quickly, so you can improve your processes continuously.

❑ The project team should establish metrics for any factor identified as being critical. Remember: "What gets measured counts" and "what gets measured gets managed."

❑ For every metric, the team should set a standard. The standard serves as the target, the criterion by which measurements are evaluated.

❑ When creating metrics, the project team must ask new questions and search for new results. It should begin with the fundamentals:

• Why do we measure this?
• Why do we measure it in this way?
• What does this measurement mean?
• Why is this measurement important?

❑ In establishing metrics, the project team should ensure that the means of measuring are going to produce data that is both *reliable* and *valid*.

❑ It's critical to link your metrics to overall performance and align them with your strategic goals. Otherwise, they can't tell you anything you really need to know.

❑ You should establish a checklist for metrics, with questions appropriate to the project and your specific situation. It should include the following general questions:
  • What are the key metrics for this process?
  • Are these metrics valid?
  • Are these metrics reliable?
  • Does everyone involved understand these metrics?
  • Do we have adequate and accurate data?
  • What is the baseline for each metric?
  • What is the goal for each metric?

People and Resources

S o far in this book, we've presented Design for Six Sigma in terms of a process and metrics. We'll cover tools in Chapters 7 and 8. But, as you know from your experience with Six Sigma, the process and all of the tools won't get you to six sigma without people to support and use the process and apply the tools. That's the focus of this chapter.

Since training and other preparation are essential to developing the people who will be responsible for DFSS projects, this chapter concludes with a section on non-human resources—books.

Key Players and the DFSS Infrastructure

Just as DFSS varies according to organizations, their business operations, their structures, and their cultures, the key players will also vary in their titles, their qualifications, their training, their roles, and their responsibilities. What follows is a general guide to the key people involved in DFSS projects:

- CEO
- Champion, aka sponsor
- Master black belts
- Black belts
- Green belts
- Team members

Executive Leaders

Success with DFSS, as with any other organizational initiative, starts at the top. Since DFSS projects involve multiple functional units and must be implemented from the top down, they must involve the CEO. As you know through your experience with Six Sigma, it's essential for the CEO to lead and support every project from beginning to end. By example, the CEO inspires commitment throughout the organization to making the most of DFSS.

Qualifications

A CEO needs no qualifications to establish and support and promote DFSS initiatives. He or she is at least minimally qualified by virtue of being the top person in the organization and ultimately responsible for all financial results of the organization. Of course, the more the CEO knows about Six Sigma, the better. If he or she has not become familiar with at least the basics through Six Sigma projects, he or she should definitely do so for DFSS.

Training and Preparation

The CEO and other executive leaders should be familiar with at least the principles and the potential of DFSS. Of course, it's also useful to know the purposes of the basic tools. Consultants, master black belts, or black belts can provide the essentials. There are also books like this one and those listed later in this chapter that can prepare executive leaders for the DFSS initiative.

The Ideal CEO

Jack Welch, the CEO who started Six Sigma at General Electric, called Six Sigma "part of the genetic code" of future leadership at that company. Welch could be considered the ideal executive leader for Six Sigma, because an executive's responsibility, ultimately, is to make sure that Six Sigma becomes part of the "genetic code" of the company. From the top down and throughout the organization, executive leaders can inspire and promote a Six Sigma culture.

Roles and Responsibilities

Here are the basic responsibilities of the CEO and other executive leaders for ensuring success with DFSS:

- **They must show *determination*.** They must believe in DFSS and be committed to making it work.
- **They must actively display *confidence*—**not only in DFSS, but also in the people responsible for making it work. They must show that they believe in their employees and support their success. Confidence is a powerful motivator.
- **They must back it all up with *integrity*.** As in all other areas, they need to do what they say they're going to do. When they follow through on their commitments and stay true to their objectives, executives demonstrate ethical leadership. Integrity inspires loyalty and respect—strong factors in motivation.
- **They must practice and model *patience*.** This is very hard in a business environment that demands instant results and immediate answers. DFSS projects take time; rushing the process will jeopardize the results.

The responsibilities listed above are generalities. Here's how they translate into actions:

- The CEO sets goals for the DFSS initiative, as an integral part of the organization's business plan.
- The CEO creates the infrastructure for the DFSS initiative. He or she sets up a management council for DFSS and serves on that council.

CAUTION!

Slow: Progress Ahead

If a company has been functioning at a four sigma level or lower for years, the leaders should be willing to allow six months—and more likely a couple of years—for projects that will bring performance up to a six sigma level. John Kotter, in his book, *Leading Change* (Cambridge, MA: Harvard Business School Press, 1996), suggests that a change of this magnitude can take up to five years. Too often, however, executives and managers are impatient for results.

Everyone may be anxious for improvement, but keep this question in mind: how much of the problem do you want to fix—all of it or just some of it? To fix it properly takes time—and patience!

- The CEO provides resources for training and support.
- The CEO gets training in DFSS.
- The CEO understands the savings that the company can achieve.
- The CEO promotes the use of metrics.
- The CEO assigns major responsibilities for the DFSS initiative and documents accountability.
- The CEO promotes DFSS. He or she may even participate actively on a DFSS team.
- The CEO ensures that project teams get the training, resources, information, and cooperation necessary for them to succeed.
- The CEO showcases achievements.
- The CEO provides recognition, rewards, and other incentives for employees who contribute to the success of DFSS projects.
- The CEO marks key milestones.
- The CEO keeps the DFSS initiative on track.
- The CEO celebrates successes.

Champion

A champion, as mentioned in Chapter 3, is generally someone selected from the ranks of upper management to serve as a leader, a mentor, and a coach, supporting the project teams and ensuring the resources necessary. The champion promotes the

Six Sigma methodology throughout the company and especially in specific functional groups. The champion understands DFSS, selects projects, establishes measurable objectives, removes barriers, and supports black belts. The champion "owns" the process—monitoring projects and measuring the savings realized.

The titles, qualifications, and responsibilities vary, usually according to the size and complexity of the organization. Owners of processes and systems who help initiate and coordinate DFSS activities in their areas of responsibilities may also be called *sponsors*. In larger organizations, the champion or sponsor may be a high-level manager, such as an executive vice president, who leads DFSS full time. There may be a champion for every key area of the organization. Also, an organization may have informal champions, people who promote the use of DFSS in their words and by their example.

Qualifications

As just mentioned, the qualifications of a champion or a sponsor vary, depending on the organization and the Six Sigma infrastructure. A champion or sponsor is often someone who's a director or a vice president. It should be someone who's responsible for developing new products or services. We might add that it helps if the champion or sponsor is "a resident crazy person," someone who dares to be different, even delighting in the role of innovator.

Training and Preparation

The champion should at least be familiar with basic and advanced statistics. It's best if he or she is trained as a black belt. The champion should also be proficient with business planning and project planning tools. He or she should be able to set goals for designing products or services, establish metrics for DFSS projects and assess their financial value, and track and demonstrate progress toward the project goals. Champions are not necessarily technical experts in Six Sigma, but rather know enough about it to coordinate DFSS projects.

Roles and Responsibilities

As mentioned in Chapter 3, the champion or sponsor is critical to any Six Sigma project. This person ensures that the project team is successful by breaking down barriers—functional, financial, personal, or other—so that the project team members can do their work. The champion does most or all of the following things:

- Selects DFSS projects.
- Establishes project goals.
- Chooses the black belts and the green belts.
- Provides direction.
- Allocates resources.
- Breaks through barriers.
- Encourages black belts and teams.
- Holds team members accountable for the project goals.
- Asks for the results.
- Ensures that the project is on track.
- Is devoted to doing whatever it takes to make the project successful.
- Interfaces with executive managers.

If the organization is large and the sponsor or champion has a greater scope of authority and responsibility, he or she may also select the executives who will serve as champions or sponsors. (Again, the use of these titles varies.)

In brief, the role of the champion is to support the DFSS process. A strong champion is vital to the success of any DFSS project.

Master Black Belts

Master black belts provide technical leadership of DFSS initiatives. They have the highest level of technical and organizational proficiency. They assist the champion, coordinate the various projects, and help the black belts when necessary. A rule of thumb is to have one MBB per 100 black belts, but in large organizations, it should be one master black belt for about every 30 black belts—and recent experience suggests that the ratio of MBBs to BBs should be closer to one for every 10.

Qualifications

People who will be serving as master black belts must be able to work with statistical and non-statistical tools, to train, and to facilitate and coordinate activities. MBBs guide and coach black belt candidates and work with champions to help them overcome obstacles. They must be able to facilitate problem-solving effectively without actually taking over a project. In addition, they provide leadership in integrating DFSS into the business strategy and operational plans of the organization. They also build relationships with organization leaders to inform about the progress of the DFSS initiative.

In selecting candidates, then, communication skills and teaching skills are as important as technical skills. Successful MBB candidates understand the applicable technologies important to the organization as well as the theory and application of the tools of DFSS. It makes sense to choose MMBs from among the top performers in the organization and to make it a path to promotion for those employees and to managerial advancement for managers who involve their people.

Training and Preparation

Master black belt is the highest level of technical proficiency. MBBs are the organization's experts on DFSS methodologies, tools, and applications in all areas and at all levels. MBBs train black belts, so they must know everything that black belts need to know. After they complete the BB training successfully, they should be trained in quantitative and qualitative analytical skills. They must also understand the theory behind the methods. MBBs must be able to help BBs apply the methods correctly in unusual situations.

Roles and Responsibilities

Master black belts focus 100% on DFSS. They focus on identifying and defining projects, teaching, mentoring, and actively working to institutionalize Six Sigma thinking. They ensure that the necessary infrastructure for DFSS is in place, they coach and mentor project teams, they train black belts, and they help train employees.

MBBs are usually assigned to a specific area of the organization, either functional or process-specific. They work closely with the owners of the process, to set goals, develop designs, and share information.

Black Belts

Black belts are the experts responsible for leading DFSS projects and teams full time. They are the key agents, fully dedicated and thoroughly trained in Six Sigma techniques and tools. Generally, each works on four to six projects a year. A rule of thumb is to have one to three BBs for every 100 employees in the organization.

Qualifications

Black belts appointed to lead DFSS projects should have a strong desire to do things differently and better, to be change agents. They should have outstanding interpersonal skills, communication skills, and facilitation skills. They should be curious. They should also be naturally strong and enthusiastic leaders held in high regard by their peers. They should be technically oriented and skilled in product development. They may come from any of a wide range of disciplines and they don't need to be trained statisticians or engineers. However, it's good if they've had college-level math, so they can handle quantitative analysis, and some education in statistical methods would be valuable.

Successful black belts generally share the following traits:

- They work well on their own and in groups.
- They remain calm under extreme pressure.

- They anticipate problems and act on them immediately.
- They respect their fellow workers and are respected by them.
- They inspire others.
- They are able to delegate tasks to other team members and coordinate their efforts.
- They understand and recognize the abilities and limitations of their fellow workers.
- They show a genuine concern for others, for what they need and want.
- They accept criticism well.
- They are concerned about the current processes and results and they want to improve the system.
- They have the intelligence and interest to learn how to apply the Six Sigma tools.

The sidebar on the next page, "Rating a Black Belt Candidate," provides an organized approach to evaluating your employees in terms of their black belt potential.

Training and Preparation

Black belts should understand operating systems, database managers, spreadsheets, presentation programs, and word processors. Their training will also require proficiency with one or more advanced statistical analysis programs, although less than with Six Sigma MAIC. (In MAIC most of the tools are statistical; in DFSS many are statistical, but many are not.) They need a solid knowledge of basic statistics, such as statistical process control, and good statistical skills. They should be familiar with the tools outlined in Chapters 7 and 8.

Training should also prepare BB candidates to lead project teams, to use DFSS methodology and tools, to coach and mentor green belts, and to mentor and advise managers on prioritizing, planning, and launching projects.

Roles and Responsibilities

Black belts must commit full time to DFSS, to achieving the

Rating a Black Belt Candidate
Here's a quick way to evaluate a potential black belt. Rate the candidate on each key characteristic, on a scale of 1 to 5 (5 = excellent, 4 = above average, 3 = average, 2 = below average, 1 = unacceptable).
Process and product knowledge _____
Basic statistical knowledge _____
Knowledge about your organization _____
Communication skills _____
Self-starter, motivated _____
Open-minded _____
Eager to learn about new ideas _____
Desire to drive change _____
Team player _____
Respected _____
Results track record _____
Total: _____
   A candidate who scores at least **38** has excellent black belt potential.

goals of their development projects. They coach and mentor project team members, manage risks, help set direction, coordinate activities, break through barriers, communicate between the teams and others in the organization, and keep the project scorecards. Although champions are responsible for the bottom-line results, since they select the projects and monitor progress, black belts are responsible for doing the work.

Green Belts

Green belts usually receive more simplified training than black belts and work on DFSS projects only part time. Depending on the organization, they generally help black belts collect data and develop experiments, they may lead small projects, or they may form DFSS teams, facilitate their work, and manage projects from start to finish. A rule of thumb is one green belt for every 20 employees.

   Developing green belts is a good means of spreading DFSS techniques and tools throughout an organization. Their level of

Smart
Managing

Shades of Black and Green

The titles "black belt" and "green belt" were first used by
Motorola—which also registered the term "Six Sigma."
These terms have become standard, more or less, but not all black
belts or green belts are the same.

Organizations and consulting firms create titles to distinguish their
Six Sigma positions from similar or same positions elsewhere. There's
also no standard for the knowledge and skills required for any of
these titles and no credentials for licensing or certifying people for
these titles. However, in 2001 the International Quality Federation
(www.iqfnet.org) started a certification program for Six Sigma black
belts.

skills and knowledge enables GBs to serve as high-performing
members on project teams.

Qualifications

Green belt candidates can be employees at virtually all levels of
the organization. Like BBs, they must be willing to do things differently and better. They should have people skills that enable
them to work as effective members of cross-functional teams
and have product development skills. They should have experience with administrative techniques and be familiar with basic
statistical tools.

Training and Preparation

Green belts usually receive simpler training than black belts.
Their training includes facilitation techniques, meeting management, project management, problem solving, exploratory data
analysis, statistics, hypothesis testing, and most of the tools
outlined in Chapters 7 and 8. This training is designed to prepare green belts to be team leaders and use DFSS methodology
and tools.

Roles and Responsibilities

Green belts spend from 10% to 50% of their time on DFSS projects, but maintain their regular work roles and responsibilities.
They generally help black belts collect and/or analyze data,

develop and conduct experiments, or do other important project tasks. They may also lead small projects or they may form DFSS teams, facilitate their work, and even manage projects from start to finish. Green belts normally concentrate on projects within their own departments.

They are team members who understand DFSS well enough to share the tools and transform the culture of the organization from the bottom up.

Team Members

Team members must have sufficient functional expertise relevant to the project and be assigned specific responsibilities. Team members must be willing to try new things.

Qualifications

Like black belts and green belts, members of project teams must be willing to participate in the DFSS process and to do things differently and better. They should be open-minded and understand that the DFSS initiative will require things of them that are very different from their traditional roles.

A Rainbow of Belts

Some organizations go beyond the black and green belts, with other color schemes. They give basic training to some employees and label them yellow belts or white belts, depending on the organization. These belts know enough about Six Sigma to gather data or to help green belts with preventing problems and applying solutions.

While the titles "black belt" and "green belt" have become fairly standard, that's not so for the titles "yellow belt" and "white belt." And there are even some organizations with brown belts (e.g., Seagate, Standard Register, and Noranda).

Finally, some organizations are getting away from all of the belts. They talk about "systems engineering," there are DFSS black belts in a support role, the development leader gets much the same training as a black belt, and the team members get much the same training as green belts.

They also must be able to work well with others and have technical skills to contribute significantly to the team. Team members can be from various functional areas affected by the DFSS project. They must have knowledge of the customers, experience with similar products or services, the authority to make decisions and commitments for the area they represent, and experience with DFSS basics.

In his *Six Sigma Project Planner* (New York: McGraw-Hill, 2003), Thomas Pyzdek suggests the following simple guidelines for evaluating candidates for a project team:

- Do they possess needed knowledge, skills, abilities, and personal attributes or certification?
- Are they willing to work on this project?
- Do they have sufficient time to work on this project?
- Will their supervisor allow their involvement?
- What is their role—sponsor, team member, advisor, process operator, process supplier, customer, interested third party?

Training and Preparation

Team members are under pressure to meet deadlines, so their training should be linked to real work. They should be trained in DFSS techniques and tools appropriate to the project and the project charter: not every member should learn everything, just what he or she can use immediately. As the techniques and tools are presented, team members should be applying them to the project.

Roles and Responsibilities

The primary responsibility of team members is to contribute technical expertise to the DFSS project, because they are selected for the team based on their functional expertise and knowledge that is relevant and sufficient to the project. Each member has specific duties and responsibilities for making the project successful. They perform tasks as delegated by the black belt leading the team.

Teamwork

It's crucial to the DFSS initiative for each black belt to get the most out of each member of his or her project team. It's important to get to know each member and to recognize what motivates him or her. Then, the black belt can take appropriate action:

- Encourage a general feeling of acceptance on the team.
- Allow social interaction among team members.
- Make individuals feel like they're valued members of the team.
- Communicate goals, objectives, and expectations.
- Give roles and duties—and the authority to perform them.
- Provide resources as needed and access to information.
- Give appropriate training and guidance.
- Empower members to make decisions.
- Recognize their contributions.
- Challenge individuals and the team as a whole.
- Encourage and promote creativity.

Bruce Tuckman developed a four-stage model to represent the natural development of teams—forming, storming, norming, and performing (Bruce W. Tuckman, "Developmental Sequence in Small Groups," *Psychological Bulletin*, vol. 63, 1965, pp. 384-399). He later added a fifth stage—adjourning (Bruce W. Tuckman and M. Jensen, "Stages of Small Group Development," *Group and Organizational Studies*, 2, 1977, pp. 419-427). Black belts and other team leaders should know what to expect and how to react, in order to guide the team members through the five stages of the natural evolution of teams:

- **Forming:** stage of transition from individuals to members of a team, characterized by enthusiasm, anxiety, idealism, and feelings of power. The leader should focus on establishing team identity, defining the project, helping members get acquainted, setting clear expectations, assigning straightforward tasks, emphasizing communication, and becoming a role model.

Smart Managing

Know What's Natural for Teams

Black belts and other team leaders should know what to expect in the five stages of team evolution:

- **Forming:** transition, enthusiasm, anxiety, idealism, and feelings of power
- **Storming:** conflicts, challenges, frustration, and disillusionment
- **Norming:** reconciliation or acceptance of differences, development of standards of behavior, productivity
- **Performing:** accomplishments, cooperation, growth, and synergy
- **Adjourning:** finalizing, concluding activities, and getting closure

- **Storming:** stage of conflicts and challenges, characterized by frustration and disillusionment. The leader should focus on resolving conflicts, creating an open atmosphere, sharing responsibility, and moving toward consensus.
- **Norming:** stage of reconciling or accepting differences, characterized by the development of standards of behavior and some productivity. The leader should focus on moving toward the project goals, fostering a sense of team spirit, and encouraging problem solving.
- **Performing:** stage of accomplishments, characterized by cooperation, growth, and synergy. The leader should focus on maintaining effective relationships, monitoring for "groupthink," communicating, evaluating and giving feedback, and celebrating achievements.
- **Adjourning:** stage of finalizing, characterized by concluding activities and getting closure. The leader should focus on evaluating results, recognizing members for their accomplishments, producing a final report, and providing a sense of closure.

Recognition and Rewards

The DFSS initiative must include recognition and rewards. The organization benefits from the results of DFSS—and so should the people who achieve those results. Rewards can be linked directly to objectives though percentages, as in any other form of gain-

The First Step Toward Teamwork

Black belts and managers working with project teams should be alert to what Patrick Lencioni terms the five *dysfunctions* (*The Five Dysfunctions of a Team: A Leadership Fable*, San Francisco: Jossey-Bass, 2002):

Absence of trust—when team members are reluctant to allow themselves to be vulnerable with each other and unwilling to admit their mistakes or any weaknesses or needs.

Fear of conflict—when members are unable to discuss and debate.

Lack of commitment—when members find it difficult to commit to decisions, when ambiguity dominates.

Avoidance of accountability—when members don't commit to taking action, when they hesitate to hold each other responsible for behaviors that are not in the best interests of the team and the project.

Inattention to results—when members tend to put their own needs ahead of the goals of the project and the team.

Without a certain comfort level among team members, a foundation of trust is impossible. Without a basic sense of trust, it's difficult or impossible to discuss or debate with any intensity. Without confrontation and conflict, it's unlikely that members will commit to decisions. Without commitment to a plan of action, there's no acceptance or expectation of accountability. Without accountability, individual needs naturally take precedence over project and team interests and goals.

Smart team leaders, therefore, begin promoting teamwork by fostering comfort among team members.

sharing. Factors in deciding the amount of reward could include the size of the project, the benefits realized, and the percentage of time devoted to the project. Cash is generally the best reward, but you could also award gift certificates and/or stock options.

Recognition is important, too, but don't expect that it will be enough—just as media publicity for your DFSS initiative would not be enough for the organization. Management expects financial benefits ... and so do those who make the initiative work.

As a manager, you should not hesitate to ask about tying compensation to your DFSS initiative. That's the only way to focus all of the people in your area on the customer and the quality of your products or services and processes.

Finally, it should be noted that the methods, collaboration, and results of the DFSS initiative foster an environment that encourages and promotes development of skills and knowledge, increases motivation, boosts morale,

> **Money Talks**
> General Electric has encouraged its executives to promote Six Sigma by linking it to compensation: 40% of the bonuses for champions is tied to Six Sigma implementation. That percentage applies to the top 7,000 executives. This incentive sends a strong message about the importance of Six Sigma and ensures commitment from the top levels down.

and empowers employees. Of course, the employees who participate on DFSS project teams also improve their chances of promotion.

Consultants

If you have a Six Sigma initiative in your organization, do you need to hire a consultant to help you with DFSS? That depends on several factors, particularly the results of the Six Sigma efforts, the complexity of the DFSS initiative, and the people in the areas to be affected. Consultants who have experience with DFSS in many organizations can help an organization get a better start on its initiative and deal better with the differences between Six Sigma and Design for Six Sigma.

How to Select a Consultant

If you decide to work with a consultant, the firm you choose should not only preach Six Sigma but also practice it. It should not be just one line of business among others. The firm should have experience with DFSS, of course, and be able to show the results it has achieved with its clients.

Check credentials. Lots of consulting firms claim to be Six Sigma experts, so you need to ask for proof of their claims. Don't settle for a sales pitch. Request references and case studies from clients. You want proof of results from their DFSS interventions.

What to Expect from a Consultant

Your consultant should direct the planning process and help you set up the infrastructure so you can move toward self-sufficiency quickly. Your consultant should help you select your DFSS projects and identify departments and people that you'll need to involve in your projects. Your consultant should train the people who will be involved in the DFSS initiatives, as necessary. The consultant can help you orchestrate all responsibilities, roles, and schedules to make a smooth transition from planning to implementation.

Your consultant can probably provide or at least recommend a project tracking system to monitor results. To ensure that your teams are meeting your objectives and that the initiative is staying on track, you should hold periodical senior reviews—formal meetings involving champions, senior leaders, and the consultant to discuss the progress of your DFSS initiative.

The consultant should focus on knowledge transfer, on showing you how to solve design problems with the most effective methods and the right tools, so you can transfer that knowledge throughout your organization.

Are They Really with You?

A good way to distinguish among consulting firms is to consider how they structure their employee reward systems. Some consultants are compensated by *time*, on the basis of billable hours. Others are compensated for *results*, on the basis of the client's return on investment.

Although both types of consultants are committed to your DFSS success, in principle, only the latter consultants are really with you, invested in your success financially, as partners.

On to Implementing

Now that we've discussed the people who will participate in your DFSS initiative, the training and preparation, and their roles and responsibilities, it's time to discuss ways to implement DFSS. As

Non-Human Resources—Books

The following selection of books on DFSS, Six Sigma, and leadership will provide good introduction to training and form a valuable supplement to organizational efforts to prepare for the DFSS initiative.

Arthur, Jay. *Six Sigma Simplified: Quantum Improvement Made Easy.* Denver, CO: LifeStar, 2000.

Barney, Matt, and Tom McCarty. *The New Six Sigma: A Leader's Guide to Achieving Rapid Business Improvement and Sustainable Results.* Upper Saddle River, NJ: Prentice Hall PTR, 2002.

Black, J. Stewart, and Hal B. Gregersen. *Leading Strategic Change.* Upper Saddle River, NJ: Financial Times Prentice Hall, 2002.

Breyfogle, Forrest W., III. *Implementing Six Sigma: Smarter Solutions Using Statistical Methods.* New York: John Wiley & Sons, Inc., 1999.

Breyfogle, Forrest W., III, James M. Cupello, and Becki Meadows. *Managing Six Sigma: A Practical Guide to Understanding, Assessing, and Implementing the Strategy That Yields Bottom-Line Success.* Milwaukee: Quality Press, 2001.

Breyfogle, Forrest W., III, David Enck, Phil Flories, and Tom Pearson. *Wisdom on the Green: Smarter Six Sigma Business Solutions,* Smarter Solutions, Inc., 2001.

Chowdhury, Subir. *Design for Six Sigma: The Revolutionary Process for Achieving Extraordinary Profits.* Chicago: Dearborn Trade Publishing, 2002.

Cohen, Lou. *Quality Function Deployment: How to Make QFD Work for You,* Reading, MA: Addison-Wesley, 1995.

Creveling, Clyde M., Jeffrey Lee Slutsky, and David Antis, Jr. *Design for Six Sigma in Technology and Product Development.* Upper Saddle River, NJ: Prentice Hall PTR, 2003.

Eckes, George. *The Six Sigma Revolution: How General Electric and Others Turned Process into Profits.* New York: John Wiley & Sons, Inc., 2001.

Eckes, George. *Making Six Sigma Last: Managing the Balance Between Cultural and Technical Change.* New York: John Wiley & Sons, 2001.

Federico, Mary, and Renee Beaty. *Rath and Strong's Six Sigma Team Pocket Guide.* New York: McGraw-Hill, 2003.

Fowlkes, William W., and Clyde M. Creveling. *Engineering Methods for Robust Product Design: Using Taguchi Methods in Technology and Product Development.* Reading, MA: Addison Wesley, 1995.

Harry, Mikel J. *The Vision of Six Sigma: A Roadmap for Breakthrough.* Phoenix, AZ: Sigma Publishing Co., 1994.

Harry, Mikel J. *The Vision of Six Sigma: Tools and Methods for Breakthrough.* Phoenix, AZ: Sigma Publishing Co., 1994.

Harry, Mikel J. *The Nature of Six Sigma Quality.* Schaumburg, IL: Motorola University Press, 1988.

Harry, Mikel J., and Richard Schroeder. *Six Sigma: The Breakthrough Management Strategy Revolutionizing the World's Top Corporations.* New York: Doubleday Currency, 2000.

Kiemele, Mark J., Stephen R. Schmidt, and Ronald J. Berdine. *Basic Statistics: Tools for Continuous Improvement.* Colorado Springs, CO: Air Academy Press, 4th ed., 1997.

Kotter, John P. *Leading Change.* Cambridge, MA: Harvard Business School Press, 1996.

Magnusson, Kjell, Dag Kroslid, and Bo Bergman. *Six Sigma: The Pragmatic Approach.* Lund, Sweden: Studentlitteratur, 2000.

Naumann, Earl, and Steven H. Hoisington. *Customer-Centered Six Sigma: Linking Customers, Process Improvement, and Financial Results.* Milwaukee: Quality Press, 2000.

Pande, Peter S., Robert P. Neuman, and Roland R. Cavanagh. *The Six Sigma Way: How GE, Motorola, and Other Top Companies Are Honing Their Performance.* New York: McGraw-Hill, 2000.

Pande, Peter S., Robert P. Neuman, and Roland R. Cavanagh. *The Six Sigma Way Fieldbook: An Implementation Guide for Process Improvement Teams.* New York: McGraw-Hill, 2001.

Perez-Wilson, Mario. *Six Sigma: Understanding the Concept, Implications, and Challenges.* Advanced Systems Consultants, 1999.

Pyzdek, Thomas. *The Six Sigma Handbook, A Complete Guide for Greenbelts, Blackbelts, and Managers at All Levels.* New York: McGraw-Hill, 2001.

Pyzdek, Thomas. *Six Sigma Project Planner.* New York: McGraw-Hill, 2003.

Rath & Strong's Six Sigma Pocket Guide. Lexington, MA: Rath & Strong, Inc., 2000.

Schmidt, Stephen R., Mark J. Kiemele, and Ronald J. Berdine. *Knowledge Based Management: Unleashing the Power of Continual Improvement.* Colorado Springs, CO: Air Academy Press, 1997.

Schmidt, Stephen R., and Robert G. Launsby. *Understanding Industrial Designed Experiments.* Colorado Springs, CO: Air Academy Press, 4th ed., 1998.

Six Sigma Academy. *The Black Belt Memory Jogger: A Pocket Guide for Six Sigma Success.* Salem, NH: GOAL/QPC, 2002.

Tennant, Geoff. *Design for Six Sigma: Launching New Products and Services Without Failure.* Aldershot, Hampshire, UK: Gower Publishing, 2002.

we mentioned earlier, for most people, what characterizes DFSS is the tools. Chapters 7 and 8 will outline the most important tools and explain why and how the teams will use them. But those tools work properly only through a process of stages and gates, within a solid infrastructure of people and resources, with appropriate objectives and metrics, and a good understanding of what to do to implement DFSS—and what *not* to do.

Manager's Checklist for Chapter 5

❏ Success with Design for Six Sigma starts at the top. It's essential for the CEO to lead and support every project from beginning to end and, by example, to inspire commitment throughout the organization to making the most of DFSS.

❏ A champion serves as a leader, a mentor, and a coach, supporting the project teams and ensuring the resources necessary. A champion promotes the Six Sigma methodology throughout the company and especially in specific functional groups.

❏ Master black belts provide technical leadership of DFSS initiatives. They assist the champion, coordinate the various projects, and help the black belts when necessary.

❏ Black belts are the experts responsible for leading DFSS projects and teams full time. They are the key agents, fully dedicated and thoroughly trained in Six Sigma techniques and tools.

❏ Green belts usually help black belts and serve as high-performing members on project teams. Developing green belts is a good means of spreading DFSS techniques and tools throughout an organization.

❏ Team members must have sufficient functional expertise relevant to the project and be assigned specific responsibilities.

❏ Consultants who have experience with DFSS in many organizations can help an organization get a better start on its initiative and deal better with the differences between Six Sigma and Design for Six Sigma. The firm should have experience with DFSS, of course, and be able to show the results it has achieved with its clients.

Implement DFSS Successfully

We've outlined the phases of DFSS in Chapter 3 and discussed the roles and responsibilities of the CEO, champion, master black belt, black belts, green belts, and team members in Chapter 5. We'll present tools in Chapters 7 and 8. But first we'll discuss how to put all of the elements together to achieve results, offering recommendations—and providing warnings.

Because Chapter 3 outlined the phases and steps of DFSS in some detail and Chapters 7 and 8 will cover the tools, this chapter will focus on what happens before, after, and outside of the phases and the activities of the project teams.

Since, as we emphasized in Chapter 5, the outcomes of DFSS depend on people, we'll organize this chapter around the people in your organization. We'll consider the CEO, executive managers, champions, master black belts, and managers. Since the responsibilities of black belts and green belts are mostly limited to the project teams, we will not include them here—although they're obviously central and essential to your DFSS initiative.

(The recommendations and warnings offered in the first part of this chapter are divided among positions and roles, but these divisions are not prescriptive. As with so much of DFSS, specific responsibilities depend on the organization and its structure and culture.)

CEOs and Executive Managers

All people at the top of the organization should be trained in at least the basics of DFSS and in implementation strategies. They should understand the strengths and recognize limitations of DFSS.

The CEOs and executive managers must answer a basic question about the DFSS initiative: How will we know if the initiative is an organizational success? The people at the top must set goals— not just financial or operational goals, but also goals for the structure and cultural of the organization, since Six Sigma involves fundamental changes. They must plan to make the transition from DFSS as an initiative to DFSS as an intrinsic part of the way the people throughout the organization think and act.

They may engage consultants and/or other experts to help with starting the DFSS initiative, but they should make sure that people at every level of the organization take ownership of the initiative. The leaders must put in place a basic strategy that includes the following:

Success Starts with Leaders

Smart Managing Mikel J. Harry, founder of Six Sigma Academy and author of *Six Sigma: The Breakthrough Management Strategy Revolutionizing the World's Top Corporations* (New York: Doubleday, 1999), stresses the importance of leadership from top management:

Leadership is 99 percent of getting Six Sigma installed. It's selling hope and then leading them [the employees] to it. Give them the vision of Oz, show them the direction it's going and then convince them you can create the yellow brick road. The rest is just civil engineering.

- A vision, stated clearly in language that everybody can understand and communicated throughout the organization
- A few key objectives that the organization must achieve to realize its vision
- A plan that aligns all activities throughout the organization with those objectives, so that each person knows how he or she should contribute toward achieving them

The leaders of the organization must be knowledgeable, committed, and involved—and their support and promotion of DFSS must be obvious, continuous, informed, and enthusiastic. They must communicate and celebrate successes. They must do whatever it takes to make sure that DFSS is not perceived as "the program of the month." They must make sure that DFSS is applied in all areas of the organization—for products, processes, and services. If they apply it at the upper levels as well as on the factory floor or in the mailroom, they're likely to convince even the skeptics.

They must select projects carefully and strategically. The initial projects should be highly visible and most likely to succeed relatively easily, to foster positive attitudes and confidence. It's best if the design project is part of a documented new product development process and the customers are defined and identified.

They should also make sure that the people selected to form the first project teams are open-minded,

---

Trouble from the Top

The big problem with Six Sigma initiatives, according to Mikel J. Harry, is at the top—senior managers are usually not trained in what constitutes a Six Sigma project and they don't link projects to organization goals.

"That tells us," he points out ("Six Sigma Survey," *Quality Digest*, January 2003), "that Six Sigma is being led by middle management and below. This happens because Six Sigma is brought in randomly across different segments of the organization in no focused way. Implementation and deployment was not rolled out from the top down. Six Sigma is starting to suffer from that."

highly skilled, and enthusiastic about being pioneers and making changes. The candidates for master black belt and black
belt should be chosen from among top performers and the CEO
and executive managers should make these roles a path to promotion for the candidates and a means of advancement for
their managers who are encouraging and supporting them.

They must also allocate sufficient resources for the projects.
If they recognize that the key to improving business is improving business processes and they align the DFSS projects with
the goals of the organization, they will understand that this
investment of resources will provide an impressive ROI.

Executive Managers

The executive managers should be committed to managing the
high-level changes that result from the DFSS initiative. They
should also help and support the champions among them.

Executives must do more than just sign the checks and
expect results. They must both lead and guide—and serve as
role models. They need to understand the principles, tools, and
implications of DFSS and they need to expect success and recognize and reward those who contribute to that success.

They must understand the difference between *deployment*
and *delegation*. Deployment requires active participation in
determining strategies, setting goals, selecting team members,
conducting phase-gate reviews, and so forth. Delegation is too
passive—and it conveys the message that the DFSS initiative is
not worth any effort from executive managers.

Executive Managers and Champions

It's crucial to the DFSS initiative to make sure that measurement systems in general and the metrics for each project align
with the overall strategies of the organization. If the organization
is going to push for reliability, for example, the executive managers and champions should make sure that reliability features
prominently among the metrics for each DFSS project.

They should also work on knowledge transfer. How can they ensure that what each project team learns gets transferred to others in the organization? How can they avoid a "silo effect" among DFSS teams?

There are software solutions available that use portal technology to allow an organization to set up portal objects, such as a newsletter or a best practices center, to share project knowledge among all employees. The same technology can be used to create a "knowledge store," where an organization can put Six Sigma and DFSS reference materials and other information, to make them available for easy access.

Also, the portal technology can be used as part of the communication plan established by the CEO and the executive managers, to deliver messages about DFSS—why it's important to the organization, how it will work, what specific people will be doing, what benefits it will bring to the various areas of the organization, how the cultural changes will help, what results have come from the initiative, and so forth.

In general, they should devise strategies for sharing and documenting lessons learned and other information. Then, they should emphasize those strategies with the champion of every project to make sure that the project plans align with those strategies for knowledge transfer.

In particular, they should monitor every project to ensure that the champion is empowering the process owner(s) to understand the changes so as to more effectively and easily assume control of the process when the project team hands over the design. Also, to ensure that design projects integrate easily, effectively, and efficiently into the operations of the organization, it's essential to help managers and employees understand DFSS and develop positive attitudes and enthusiastic acceptance of changes.

The executive managers and champions should be the guardians of the phase-gate reviews. As mentioned earlier in the book, the phases of DFSS are not carved in stone. They vary according to the organization, the project, and the environment.

The key to success is specific and rigorous phase-gate reviews that are appropriate to the project and its objectives. Good reviews flatten out the "worry curve" and ensure that projects remain on track.

Each gate should have clearly defined deliverables with descriptions. These deliverables should include knowledge transfer, so that it's one of the responsibilities for every team for every phase of every project.

The executive managers should work with the champions to make the gate review and signoff process consistent. The focus should be on reporting on the major risks of the project and critical decisions to be made; teams should not present reams of data. The champions should understand that they must require teams to provide knowledge and results and that reviews should provide managers with the information they need in order to decide whether to sign off.

The executive managers must also emphasize with the champions that they should adjust expectations as a project progresses. That means throwing out deliverables that add no value to the project and/or adding new deliverables where there's clear need for them.

Finally, the executive managers and champions must ensure that managers and others who are responsible for attending reviews take that responsibility seriously, that it be a top priority for them, and that managers respect the signoff process and expect the teams to achieve their goals for each phase of their projects.

Champions

No DFSS project will be successful without a strong champion or sponsor. This person—generally the executive manager responsible for the new product or service being designed— must have the authority to make things happen for the project team—and then use that authority to support the team and facilitate the project.

The champion must obtain resources for the project. The champion must protect the team by balancing competing priorities and warding off pressures. The champion must serve as the team liaison with upper management. The champion must monitor the project and ensure that it stays on track.

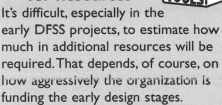

Rule of Thumb for Resources

It's difficult, especially in the early DFSS projects, to estimate how much in additional resources will be required. That depends, of course, on how aggressively the organization is funding the early design stages.

However, as a rule of thumb, experts recommend allocating 15% to 25% beyond your current funding level at the early design stages.

Champions should be trained so they understand at least the basic DFSS tools and their purposes. They should also be very familiar and comfortable with the unique roles and responsibilities of the champion and know how the master black

Enough Is Enough!

The champion should take responsibility for freezing requirements, allowing the team to stop adding to the specifications for a product or a process and moving on with the design. In "Straight Talk on DFSS" (*Six Sigma Forum Magazine*, August 2002), Charles Huber and Robert Launsby tell the following story.

The latter was a program manager for a flexible disk product line in the early '80s. The technical requirements for the product were well-defined, as they were determined by the disk drive design—but not the packaging and labeling requirements.

The market requirements person was working hard to understand the marketplace, so every two weeks he would visit another customer—and bring back dozens of packaging requests, which he wanted to add to the product specifications. He continued to make those requests late in the design effort.

The project would have been more successful if all employees in contact with the customers had gotten their requirements early in the design cycle.

"Unfortunately," the authors conclude, "even today this example is standard operating procedure in numerous organizations ... and evolving requirements are a major barrier to effectively implementing DFSS."

belts, the black belts, the green belts, and the other members of the project team depend on them. They should help with establishing and promoting a common vocabulary, so people throughout the organization understand better and more easily across all projects.

Champions should know that training should be practical, just in time, and applied to the project. They should make sure that master black belts and black belts take that approach to training and explain a tool just before the team will be using it, so team members learn better and understand immediately why and how the tool works.

In selecting members for project teams, champions should choose employees from all of the functions to be directly affected by the product or service targeted. The team members should be open to new approaches and to change and they should be enthusiastic about being part of something new and exciting, pioneers for the organization. The champion should then ensure, from the start, that all of the players know what specific roles they play on the team.

In selecting black belts for DFSS projects, champions should choose employees who are willing to commit full time to DFSS and are willing, even eager, to break through barriers. For each project, the champion should emphasize the objectives and what is expected of the team for each phase-gate review—and then enforce those expectations at the reviews.

Champions should work with managers to involve employees in the DFSS process and to keep them informed of progress and changes. That way, it should be easier for employees to understand the changes and accept them. It's smart to know what they need or how improvements will benefit them, to help them realize that the advantages are greater than the discomforts of change.

Managers

Managers at all levels should show that they're committed to DFSS. By discussing it with their employees and being positive about the results of projects, they can help promote the initiative and prepare their employees for the changes.

A manager should get actively involved if there's a project that will affect his or her specific area. He or she should make a point of talking with the new project team members, particularly in the early phases of deployment, to show interest and support.

Obstacles

In their *Introduction to Six Sigma: A Practitioner's Guide to Learning and Implementing Six Sigma* (http://filebox.vt.edu/users/mckinnon/Introduction%20to%20Six%20Sigma.htm), Ritesh Mahna, Tanicka L. McKinnon, and Brian Seward list obstacles encountered by organizations as they implement Six Sigma:

- Inability to inspire and train employees and gain complete participation
- Inability to link Six Sigma goals to profits
- Inability to link Six Sigma goals with optimum levels of resource utilization
- Inability to integrate Six Sigma into the supply chain
- Overemphasis on costs
- Resistance to the Six Sigma initiative (incompetence, issues of control and ownership, fear, emotional issues)

Their conclusions may surprise you:

Many of these issues deal with managing the human element of business. Management's inactivity is what creates the most hurdles. Also, management has to be committed to the cause of the methodology. Then there will always be insight needed from management to link the Six Sigma initiatives to the bottom line.

They emphasize the importance of paying attention to the human issues involved. The two primary problems are resistance from employees unable to adapt to the technology of Six Sigma, because of inadequate training, and resistance from line managers to changes that threaten their sense of control over resources that are diverted to the Six Sigma initiative.

They offer the following recommendations:

- Align projects with overall organizational goals.
- Understand that Six Sigma is more than just a statistical tool, that it's a "structured application of statistical and managerial techniques and concepts."
- Involve suppliers and customers in the Six Sigma initiative, since the approach can be effective throughout the supply chain.
- Keep Six Sigma focused on customers.

Causes of Failure

Mike Carnell, president of Six Sigma Applications and co-author of *Leaning into Six Sigma* (New York: McGraw-Hill, 2003), recently compiled two lists of reasons why Six Sigma deployments have failed to meet expectations ("Understanding Six Sigma Deployment Failures," www.isixsigma.com/library/content/c020916a.asp). All of the causes of failure would fit under the heading "User Errors" and are not due to any "defects" in Six Sigma.

Carnell first lists ways in which master black belts, black belts, and green belts have caused results of Six Sigma projects to be less than expected:

- They did not leave their other jobs behind, at least through training.
- They treated Six Sigma as an academic exercise.
- They failed to appreciate the complexity of dealing with people.
- They spent too much time running computer programs and not enough time in the process.
- They avoided resistance, not dealing with it when they recognized it.
- They appealed to the champion to break through a barrier rather than trying to do it themselves.

- They did not appeal to the champion to break through a barrier after than trying to do it themselves.
- They created an "exclusive club attitude" around the Six Sigma program.
- They did not transfer ownership of the solution to the team as the project progressed. In other words, it became a personal possession.
- They focused on gaining certification rather than on the project and the results for the organization.
- They did not get at least a basic understanding of the tools required to do an analysis.
- They generated false data.
- They did not communicate effectively with management—in the language of money.
- They presented results as reporting on a science project, using piles of figures rather than graphics to convey results.
- They covered a lack of content in presentations and/or project reviews with slides and/or special effects.
- They failed to recognize the final phase—Control—as the most difficult.
- They did not share credit with the project team or allow the team the opportunity to share the spotlight by attending management presentations or collaborating in presentations.
- They took credit for work accomplished by another project team.

Many of the problems listed by Carnell could be avoided if champions followed the projects more closely, emphasized the importance of training for all members of the project teams, and promoted teamwork and communication.

The second list that Carnell presents is of ways in which champions and other managers, particularly at the upper levels, have caused Six Sigma projects to be less successful:

- There was a prevailing belief that a single initiative would solve all problems in the organization.
- There was no concept of customer expectations.
- There was no vision related to customer expectations.
- There was no visible leadership at the executive level.
- There was little or no alignment (horizontal or vertical) of Six Sigma.
- Senior management tried to change the organization without a detailed change process.
- There was no follow-up on the annual operating plan.
- Six Sigma was deployed without a reason.
- Six Sigma was deployed with no plan for attaining the goal.
- The deployment plan was delegated to a consulting company.
- There were no plans to deploy Six Sigma into design and marketing after deploying in operations.
- Deployment plans were not communicated effectively through the organization.
- The project selection process did not identify projects related to business objectives.
- There was no queue of projects for master black belts, black belts, and green belts, to move them along from a completed project to a new project.
- There were no metrics in place for management participation.
- There were no metrics for champions.
- There was limited or no feedback on metrics.
- There was no accountability.
- Executives did not make it a priority to show up for report meetings.
- Champions did not make it a priority to show up for report meetings.
- Middle managers continued following their own agendas, as if support of Six Sigma projects was optional.
- Champions did not break through barriers.

- Process owners did not buy into the initiative.
- Black belts were trained without computers.
- The software provided for the initiative was inexpensive and inadequate.
- There was no rewards or recognition program.
- The rewards or recognition program did not recognize teams.
- There was no program to retain employees trained in Six Sigma.
- Management tried to use contractual agreements to retain master black belts and black belts.
- The suppliers were providing poor-quality materials.
- Black belts were used to fight fires.

As you read through this list of problems, you may be concluding that most of the problems could be prevented if the CEO and executive managers understood Six Sigma better, committed to the initiative more fully and for the duration, planned for implementation and for success, and assigned responsibilities and enforced accountability at all levels.

Recommendations

How can managers minimize problems in implementing DFSS? Here are some recommendations from Ritesh Chatterjee, Six Sigma Leader for Owens Corning India Ltd. ("Top 10 Tips For Managing Six Sigma," www.isixsigma.com/library/content /c021030a.asp).

1. Commitment from the leaders and top managers is essential. They should be introduced to Six Sigma and trained in the tools and techniques and in the roles and responsibilities of managers as champions. Also, the executive managers should form a steering committee, to ensure that Six Sigma projects are aligned with organizational goals, resources are allocated, and barriers are removed.
2. All leaders should be trained to be champions. This training should ensure that the champions know how to ask

the right questions of consultants, master black belts, black belts, and green belts.

3. Six Sigma planning must be included in the operating plan.
4. Select the right consultant. Find someone who is a black belt or master black belt to provide training, a practitioner rather than an academic, so the focus is on application.
5. Ensure a Return on Training Investment of at least 20 times, through properly defining the projects and assigning the right people to project teams.
6. Start the movement at the bottom level. Train the people who are responsible for the processes—shop floor operators or customer service staff or whoever it may be—and their supervisors in the use of tools and techniques. Establish ownership and responsibility. Reward the project leaders and their team members appropriately.
7. Create a certification process. It should be rigorous, to ensure that candidates demonstrate the proper use of tools and techniques and complete projects successfully.

Six Best Practices

Vince Fayad, director of Value-Based Six Sigma for ITT Industries, Inc., attributes the success of the program primarily to six best practices ("Best Practices—ITT Champions Six Sigma," *Industry Week*, April 1, 2002):

- Link projects to the strategic plan. Decide where you want a part of the organization to be in the future and then pick projects that will help it get there.
- Go for quick wins. Select projects that can succeed in little time. Quick success generates enthusiasm for the initiative and energizes people.
- Match projects and resources. Don't yield to the natural tendency to try to do a lot of projects at one time.
- Secure support from management. Senior managers must be committed to the DFSS initiative and to facilitating work on projects.
- Provide training for top managers. When executives understand what the DFSS players are doing, they're likely to take their own responsibilities for the initiative more seriously.
- Recognize, reward, and share successes.

8. Develop a process for experienced practitioners to mentor new candidates after training.
9. Validate the financial returns of projects. The finance department should reporting on the metrics and savings in the Control phase of each project. The project leader or process owner should then continue to track the project metrics.
10. Do not allow Six Sigma to be classified as the responsibility of the quality manager. Create an infrastructure for the Six Sigma initiative and assign roles and responsibilities throughout the organization.

Lessons Learned

It seems appropriate to close this chapter of recommendations and warnings with a list of lessons learned from implementing DFSS, compiled by David Treichler, Ronald Carmichael, Antone Lusmanoff, John Lewis, and Gwendolyn Berthiez ("Design for Six Sigma: 15 Lessons Learned," *Quality Progress*, 35:1, January 2002).

1. To achieve world-class quality requires careful preparation and a commitment to making fundamental changes.
2. DFSS generates profits in direct proportion to the size of the investment: the greater the initial investment in eliminating design problems, the greater the profits throughout the life cycle.

Soft Is Hard

The following comments made in a forum on Six Sigma should guide managers:

Mindset is certainly the key ... factor in the success of Six Sigma. Knowing the techniques is not enough! ...The "soft" issues are the most difficult, critical, challenging, frustrating and even interesting issues. We're good at identifying problems, root causes, redesigning processes, and moving people around on the org chart, but the lack of sustainable results always goes back to the people and the extent to which they resist change.

---

3. The financial impact of DFSS is significantly improved if there is a structured compensation system that rewards leadership and cooperation in the DFSS initiative.
4. To ensure appropriate levels of commitment, leaders—especially middle managers—must be chosen, prepared, and trained much earlier in the process.
5. Everybody in the organization must accept and support DFSS as an integral part of doing business that requires adequate money, time, and resources.
6. The organization must treat customers as partners and continually get input from them.
7. DFSS must include everybody in the organization and become an essential principle. Employees and managers must understand DFSS and the benefits for the customers, the organizations, and everybody in it.
8. The organization must "drive product and process compatibility across the entire value chain and product life cycle."
9. Suppliers and subcontractors must be integrated into the DFSS activity, because they are part of the value chain for customers.
10. DFSS project teams must not allow new designs to cause new variability in products or processes.
11. Metrics must "capture, explain, and track improvement and performance at every level of the organization" and be integrated into the strategic plan.
12. DFS can apply in diverse industries, "if the design and production application is integrated and balanced."
13. Organizations are suffering from a loss of knowledge and a lack of experience and skills. This hampers the teams: it's difficult to meet schedules, conduct thorough statistical analysis and introduce rapid change.
14. Expanding the responsibility for design, so project team members follow a design from beginning to end, promotes ownership that changes the approach to product design.

15. The trend toward engineering efficiency ... has made engineers a commodity ... when the loss of domain knowledge
makes the need for longevity in an organization essential.

Manager's Checklist for Chapter 6

❏ All people at the top of the organization should be trained in
at least the basics of DFSS and in implementation strategies,
to understand its strengths and recognize its limitations.

❏ The leaders must put in place a basic strategy that includes
the following:
  • A vision, stated clearly in language that everybody can
    understand and communicated throughout the organiza-
    tion
  • A few key objectives that the organization must achieve
    to realize its vision
  • A plan that aligns all activities throughout the organization
    with those objectives, so that each person knows how he
    or she should contribute toward achieving them

❏ It's crucial to the DFSS initiative to make sure that measurement systems in general and the metrics for each project
align with the overall strategies of the organization.

❏ No DFSS project will be successful without a strong champion or sponsor. This person must have the authority to make
things happen for the project team—and then use that
authority to support the team and facilitate the project.

❏ Managers at all levels should show that they're committed to
DFSS. By discussing it with their employees and being positive about the results of projects, they can help promote the
initiative and prepare their employees for the changes.

DFSS Tools, Part 1

What are the main tools used in DFSS? That's a huge question and impossible to answer. DFSS places strong emphasis on customer analysis, the transition of customer needs and requirements down to process requirements, and minimizing defects, costs, and time. A few tools are common to any DFSS methodology, but the use of other tools will vary according to whether the design is of a product or a service or a process, the specific context, and the priorities.

A book of this scope cannot present all of the DFSS tools in sufficient detail. Most of the tools in this chapter and the next easily warrant a chapter in itself. In fact, some of these have filled books. Our purpose here is simply to provide brief explanations of the more important DFSS tools used generally. The tools are presented here in more or less a usual way to use them, although the order in which tools are used varies according to the version of DFSS, the project, and the context, although—as we've noted in Chapter 3—some tools are useful throughout the DFSS process.

To go beyond what we present here, perhaps the best two resources—other than your MBB and BBs—are two books by Thomas Pyzdek—*The Six Sigma Handbook* (McGraw-Hill, 2000) and *The Six Sigma Project Planner* (McGraw-Hill, 2003)— and *Design for Six Sigma in Technology and Product Development* by Clyde M. Creveling, Jeffrey Lee Slutsky, and David Antis Jr. (Prentice Hall, 2002).

Phase-Gate Project Reviews

As mentioned in Chapter 3, it's important to set up for each phase of a new project a *phase-gate review*, also known as a *stage-gate review*, a *project review*, a *phase review*, a *project tollgate review*, or a *project milestone review*. Through this mechanism, a multi-functional management team, often consisting of vice presidents or directors, reviews and assesses the project at the end of each phase. According to the plan set forth in the project charter and the criteria defined for the project, the managers review timelines, check deliverables, and then decide whether or not the project is successful enough to merit further expenditure of resources.

Each stage-gate review should have well-defined entry criteria or deliverables, an objective, and an agenda. And all members of the project team should understand the purposes of the reviews and prepare for them appropriately. Not only must the phase-gate process be set up but the organization also needs to have the discipline to use the process. We frequently find organizations that have processes that are thought through and documented well, but do not rigorously use them. If an activity is identified as being necessary to complete a phase, then it should be done— and not waived, as we sometimes see.

Charles Waxer, in "Successful Six Sigma Project Reviews" (www.isixsigma.com/library/content/c010520a.asp), emphasizes the importance of communication in Six Sigma projects: "Communication starts with the project charter and lives through project reviews."

He states that project reviews are "simply status checks"—occasions for evaluating the status of the project relative to the plan set forth in the project charter, reviewing timelines, validating proper use of Six Sigma tools, and monitoring key progress deliverables.

He offers the following list of suggestions for the team leader, to ensure gaining maximum benefits from the review:

- **Monitor the progress of the project.** Make sure that all members of the team are focused on the phase objectives and working together.
- **Provide guidance.** A good leader guides the team members without giving the impression of doubting their competence and undermining their confidence and morale.
- **Align activities with the objectives.** Working together necessitates communication among team members, to make sure that all are making appropriate progress.
- **Show support.** The team leader motivates and energizes team members by facilitating and providing advice resources.
- **Eliminate obstacles.** Project reviews allow the opportunity for team members to identify obstacles for the champion to eliminate.
- **Share lessons learned.** Team members and leaders of other project teams can share and discuss ways to work more effectively and efficiently.
- **Recognize results.** Treat each phase as a mini project and progress as a partial success and recognize the team members for their contributions.

It's sometimes necessary to kill a project. Sometimes a project that looked good early on turns out to have flaws. Many organizations have a very difficult time dropping projects. But killing a project early is smarter than putting a "dog" out in the marketplace.

Benchmarking

Benchmarking in DFSS can be part of selecting a project and also a means of eliminating potential failure modes from the design. As mentioned in Chapter 4, there are basically three types of benchmarking:

- internal—identifying the best business practices within your own organization and sharing them across the functional areas
- competitive—researching the products, services, and processes of direct and/or best-in-class competitors, to identify and describe them as a basis of comparison for your own products, services, and processes
- functional—Identifying and examining the activities of organizations considered to be the best in class in some function

As noted in Chapter 3, benchmarking best practices may not help in developing a design, and may actually hurt, since sometimes comparisons—even with the best—can hinder creativity. Knowing that something is the best can be intimidating.

Measurement System Analysis

Good measurement is absolutely fundamental to Six Sigma projects. When the project team identifies channels for process capability data, it should conduct a measurement system analysis (MSA) on the means of measuring process capability. After all, if you do not ensure that your measurement system is both accurate and precise each and every time it is used, 100% of the time, you risk working with flawed data. And your results are only as good as your data.

There are three key concepts in measurement:

- Validity: A measurement or a method of measuring is valid if it represents the measured feature usefully or appropriately.

- Precision: A measurement or a method of measuring is precise if repeated measurements of the same feature vary little or not at all.
- Accuracy: A measurement or a method of measuring is accurate (or unbiased) if measurements on average produce true or correct values.

Precision is largely an intrinsic property of a measurement method or device. There is not really any way to adjust for poor precision or to remedy it except to overhaul or replace measurement technology or to average multiple measurements.

As discussed in Chapter 3, MSA consists of procedures using an experimental, mathematical method for detecting and quantifying the extent to which any variation within the measurement process contributes to overall process variability. An MSA generally involves the following factors:

- **repeatability:** The degree of variation among repeated measurements, the ability of an instrument to reproduce a reading with certain accuracy.
- **reproducibility:** The degree of variation in the averages among appraisers repeatedly measuring the same characteristic of a single part.
- **stability:** The degree of variation in measurements when a known, constant input (a single characteristic) is measured over an extended time span.
- **linearity:** The difference in the bias values or repeatability across the expected operating range of the measuring instrument, consistency.
- **bias:** The difference between the observed average of measurements and the reference value. This offset or drift from "zero" necessitates adding a consistent "bias factor" to all measurements.
- **discrimination:** The ability to distinguish differences, which requires enough increments for differences to be measured. It's ideal to have 10 possible values between limits; it's only marginally useful to have five possible val-

> ## How Much Is Too Much?
> Acceptability of measurement errors revealed through
> MSA will depend on many factors, particularly the nature of
> the specifications and the customer. But you should be familiar with
> any guidelines used in your specific industry. Here, for example, are the
> guidelines for measurement system acceptability advocated by the
> Automotive Industry Action Group (AIAG):
> * under 10% error is acceptable
> * 10% to 30% error is acceptable depending on the importance of
>   application, the cost of measurement device, the cost of repair, and
>   other factors
> * over 30% error is unacceptable: and you should improve your
>   measurement system

ues; and it's impossible to allow for adequate discrimination with fewer possible values.

Voice of the Customer (VOC)

Design should begin with the customers. DFSS focuses on determining what customers require and value.

"Voice of the customer" (VOC) is a term that describes stated and unstated customer needs or requirements. It's important to keep in mind that customer voices are diverse. Within any organization, there are multiple customer voices: the procuring unit, the user, and the supporting maintenance unit. Within any of those units, there may also be multiple customer voices. The project team must consider these diverse voices in developing designs.

As mentioned in Chapter 3, there are many ways to capture the voice of the customer (VOC)—surveys, focus groups, one-on-one interviews, contextual inquiry, customer specifications, field reports, complaint logs, conjoint analysis .... The next step is to process that input, to document, organize, and analyze the information—and, again, project teams have a wide range of tools from which to choose. Here we'll touch upon only a few of these.

Customer Survey Analysis

A survey is used to gather information from a sample of individuals, usually a fraction of the population being studied. In a bona fide survey, the sample is scientifically chosen so that each person in the population will have a measurable chance of selection. Surveys can be conducted in various ways, including over the telephone, by mail, and in person. Focus groups and one-on-one interviews are popular types of in-person surveys.

Without surveying the customers adequately, it's difficult to know which features of a product or a service will contribute to its success or failure—or to understand why.

A well-designed customer survey should ask:

- What was expected or wanted?
- What was experienced?
- What is your level of satisfaction with the product?
- What is the degree of relative importance of this variable?

Surveys are useful in some situations, but they're weak in terms of getting the types of data necessary for a new design. That's why teams are using *contextual inquiry*, a newly popular approach to getting at root customer needs.

Contextual inquiry, as defined in Chapter 3, is a structured qualitative market research method that uses a combination of techniques to discover customer needs through observing and interviewing people in the context of using the product or service. Briefly, contextual inquiry involves having small teams observe how customers or potential customers interact with products. (This is sometimes referred to as "living with the customer.") The team makes notes of the likes, dislikes, and frustrations that arise from these interactions. Customers can be very helpful in providing technical solutions to problems they're experiencing. It's important to make note of any technical solution. However, typically customers do not know what the best technical solutions are, so it's better to leave that up to your engineers. But make sure they grasp the fundamental, underlying need that the customers want satisfied.

Affinity Diagramming

After the project team has gathered information on customer requirements and expectations, it needs to organize the information. If it needs to consolidate disparate items from interview notes, survey results, market research, and so forth into a selection of essential statements, affinity diagramming can be a useful tool. Team members transcribe onto cards brief statements of customer requirements and expectations. They then organize these cards into logical groupings of related needs. This makes it easier to identify similarities and redundancies and ensure that key needs are represented. This is also known as the KJ method, after its inventor, anthropologist Kawakita Jiro.

Quality Function Deployment (QFD)

Quality function deployment (QFD) is a natural part of most DFSS strategies. It's a systematic approach for transitioning VOC into design requirements. The project team uses QFD to translate what customers need and want into critical technical characteristics and ultimately into critical-to-quality characteristics (CTQs) at each stage, from research through to marketing, sales, and distribution.

QFD was developed in the late 1960s in Japan by Professors Shigeru Mizuno and Yoji Akao. Statistical quality control was gaining acceptance as a means of improving quality. Mizuno and Akao wanted to develop a quality assurance method to apply in the design process.

To benefit more fully from QFD analysis, the project team begins with the Kano model, then uses the VOC table (VOCT), and follows up with the house of quality (HOQ).

Kano Model

Developed in the 1980s by Professor Noriaki Kano, the Kano model is based on concepts of customer quality and provides a simple ranking system that distinguishes between essential and differentiating attributes. Simply put, the Kano Model is used to assess levels of customer satisfaction.

It's a conceptual model for understanding that customers have a range of requirements for any product or service. It divides those requirements into three categories, according to customer input on Kano questionnaires:

- basic requirements (unspoken), dissatisfiers
- variable requirements (spoken), satisfiers
- excitement attributes (unspoken), latent requirements, delighters

Basic requirements must be present in order for the product to be successful. These minimum requirements can be viewed as the price of entry. *Variable requirements* are directly correlated with customer satisfaction. Attributes in this category will please the customer more or less depending on the degree to which they are present in the product or service. Finally, *excitement attributes* are features that go beyond what customers might ordinarily expect, that give them great satisfaction, and for which they're willing to pay a premium price. In designing a product or a service, the DFSS team must account for all three categories to ensure a successful business strategy.

Kano model A diagram in the form of a cross in which each customer requirement for a product or a service is placed in one of three classes: basic requirements or dissatisfiers, variable requirements or satisfiers, and excitement attributes or latent requirements or delighters. This method was devised by quality expert Noriaki Kano.

According to the Kano Model, not all characteristics are equal in the eyes of the customer. Furthermore, just responding to customer complaints and spoken requirements is not enough. We must be proactive in seeking out customer needs and we must remain aware that those needs will change over time.

Voice of the Customer Table

This tool allows a project team to record information about cus-

Driving Forces

If you're designing a car, you might consider the following among hundreds of features:

- engine, brakes, wheels: basic requirements or dissatisfiers—A car must have these minimum features or customers will be dissatisfied.
- price, performance, choices of color: variable requirements or satisfiers—A car will satisfy customers more or less according to how low it's priced, how well it performs, and how many colors the company offers.
- talking controls, satellite navigation system: latent requirements or delighters—A car will delight or excite customers if it offers either or both of these features.

tomer needs in a way that captures the context of those needs to enable the team to better understand explicit and implicit customer requirements. VOCT is not only useful for recording information about customer needs in context, but it also serves as a preliminary exercise before the team builds a QFD house of quality.

For each customer statement, the team enters a customer I.D. and demographic information (sex, age, location, etc.) and information about product or service use. The information is categorized in terms of basic questions—what, when, where, why, how—that provide a context for analyzing and understanding the customer statements. The team also indicates "external" and "internal," to distinguish between information gathered directly from customers and information generated within the organization. (See Figure 7-1.) The second part of the VOC table is for translating statements into requirements.

House of Quality

The house of quality (HOQ) helps the team members structure their thinking, reach a consensus about where to focus the attention of the organization, and communicate this information throughout the organization. This tool helps ensure that they don't leave anything out when they identify CTQs that are the source of customer satisfaction (in contrast with FMEA, in

ID	Demographic	Voice of the Customer	Use									
			What		When		Where		Why		How	
			I/E	Data	I/E	Data	I/E	Data	I/E	Data	I/E	Data

Reworded Data	Quality Demanded	Quality Characteristic	Function	Reliability	Comment

Figure 7-1. Voice of the customer table
Source: *Quality Function Deployment: How to Make QFD Work for You*, by Lou Cohen (Boston: Addison-Wesley, 1995, p. 78)

which they identify CTQs that are the source of customer dissatisfaction), at the system level, subsystem levels, and components level.

The HOQ is a process for ensuring that customer needs drive the entire development process, a tool for planning and organizing CTQs at all levels of the design, and a method for providing early focus and alignment for the development team. It's an L-shaped matrix that allows a project team to quantitatively analyze the relationship between customer needs and design attributes. The HOQ is an assembly of deployment hierarchies and tables:

- the Demanded Quality Hierarchy (rows)
- the Quality Characteristics Hierarchy (columns)
- the relationships matrix (which uses one of several distribution methods) (roof)

- the Quality Planning Table (room at right)
- the Design Planning Table (bottom room)

There are four key phases in the HOQ (the first phase of QFD):

- **Phase 1. Product Planning:** Translate what the customer wants into prioritized design requirements or top company measures.
- **Phase 2. Part Planning:** Translate design requirements or company measures from phase 1 into part characteristics.
- **Phase 3. Process Planning:** Translate part characteristics from phase 2 into key process characteristics that optimize the design.
- **Phase 4. Production Planning:** Translate process characteristics from phase 3 into production and process requirements that will maximize your ability to provide the product or the service most efficiently.

QFD: Current Use and Potential

QFD is a valuable tool for ensuring that customer needs drive the entire design development process. It's effective for focusing and aligning the project team very early in the Identify phase of DFSS, identifying gaps and targets, and planning and organizing requirements at all levels of the design.

We find many organizations have had bad experiences with QFD. Here are recommendations for avoiding some common errors we've seen in the use of QFD:

- Don't assume you already know customer needs and skip the Concept Engineering steps.
- Don't assume you already know customer importance of CTC and decide not to survey customers for this information.
- Make sure your project teams are cross-functional.
- Make sure to do "the roof" of the house of quality.
- Don't mix up CTQs and CTCs.

- Don't use CTQs that are not measurable.
- Don't attempt to conduct initial QFDs without a skilled facilitator.
- Don't itemize every item in the QFD. A rule of thumb is to limit your items to 20 x 20. In *Design for Six Sigma in Technology and Product Development,* Clyde Creveling, Jeffrey Lee Slutsky, and David Antis, Jr. suggest *NUD*, considering only *new, unique,* and *difficult* items in the QFD.

Project teams could make even greater use of QFD, according to two advocates. Stefan Schurr, MD of Qualica Software GmbH of Munich, Germany, and Craig T. Smith, vice president of Rath & Strong, recently proposed a more comprehensive QFD approach ("Using Comprehensive QFD Including Function, Reliability, and Cost as the Backbone for a Design for Six Sigma Strategy," International Symposium on QFD 2002).

They suggest using a system of 15 matrices to integrate and link QFD with Six Sigma scorecards, TRIZ, value analysis, analytic hierarchy process, experiment planning, functional analysis, target costing, New Concept Selection, and matrix-based FMEA. (Bob King of GOAL/QPC was using a version of this "matrix of matrices" in the early 1980s.)

Schurr and Smth suggest that when a project team builds a system of matrices to document relationships between needs and solutions, QFD becomes "a repository of product planning knowledge forming the central nervous system of DFSS." QFD and DFSS together can add control to any design process to ensure continually meeting customer requirements.

Analytic Hierarchy Process (AHP)

The Analytic Hierarchy Process is a tool for multi-criteria analysis that enables people to explicitly rank tangible and intangible factors against each other in order to establish priorities.

The first step is to decide on the relative importance of the criteria, comparing each one against each of the others. Then, some simple calculations determine the weight that will be assigned to each criterion: this weight will be between 0 and 1 and the weights of all criteria will total to 1.

The second step is to evaluate each factor on each criterion. All options are paired separately for each criterion, for comparison. Users are often encouraged to express comparisons through verbal statements that express relative merit or interest: e.g., "In terms of [criterion], how many times more is option A preferable to option B or option B preferable to option A?"

These paired comparisons of options and of criteria are then subjected to matrix mathematics, which assigns numbers ("weights") to both the options and the criteria to show priorities.

This tool, developed by mathematician Thomas L. Saaty, a professor at the University of Pittsburgh and author of *The Analytic Hierarchy Process* (New York; London: McGraw-Hill International, 1980), consists of four steps:

1. The decision problem is broken down into criteria and factors.
2. Criteria are evaluated.
3. Factors are evaluated among themselves in terms of the criteria.
4. The priorities are synthesized.

This tool for multi-criteria analysis has another benefit for DFSS project teams. By breaking down the steps in the selection process, AHP reveals the extent to which team members understand and can evaluate factors and criteria. The team leaders can use it to stimulate discussion of alternatives.

DFSS Scorecards

Scorecards provide a systematic way for the project team to do the following:

- Set goals.
- Predict results.
- Calculate capability.

- Identify gaps.
- Track performance as progress toward the goals.

Computer programs allow a project team to create scorecards that fit the specifics of any particular project and context. DFSS scorecards generally include at least the following headings:

- CTQ
- items and component items
- base DPM
- improve %
- goal DPM
- data (Y/N)
- source
- data DPM

For designs that consist of several levels, the team may need hierarchical scorecards, consisting of several levels of scorecards. The basic scorecard might break down into an input variables scorecard and a supplier scorecard, for example. Figure 7-2 shows an example of scorecard.

Pugh Concept Selection Technique

For evaluating design alternatives, a project team can make two passes. The first evaluation is centered on the Pugh concept selection technique: the team selects the best alternatives or improves upon them. On the second pass, the team uses concept FMEA. FMEA should be done concurrently with Pugh, but just on the last few design concepts in the step just before convergence. FMEA takes time; using the above approach, the team needs to do FMEA only on the final few concepts.

The Pugh concept selection technique is a method for concept selection using a scoring matrix called the *Pugh matrix* or the *criteria-based matrix*. This is a form of prioritization matrix usually associated with the QFD method.

This technique, also known as *concept screening,* is based on a method developed by the late Stuart Pugh in the 1980s (*Total*

| Project: Structural Analysis | | | | | | | | | | | Analyst: JJM | | | Date: 5/5/03 | | | |

Input V	Units	T.F. Y/N	Lower Spec	Target Mean	Upper Spec	Term S or L	Size	Mean	Sample St Dev	Z_{ST}	DPM_{LT}	Mean	St Dev	Z_{ST}	DPM_{LT}
Margin	Kg	Yes	0	9831.85								9831.85	5396.91	3.32	34246.1

Figure 7-2. DFSS scorecard

Design: Integrated Methods for Successful Product Engineering, Boston: Addison-Wesley, 1991). It is an iterative evaluation method in which options are assigned scores relative to criteria; the selection is then made based on the consolidated scores. The Pugh technique is effective for comparing alternative concepts—and most effective if each member of the team performs it independently and the team then compares the results.

Here are the steps for applying the Pugh concept selection technique (Figure 7-3):

1. Select the requirements, the evaluation criteria.
2. Individual team members or small groups form lists of 10-20 criteria. These are frequently based upon the technical requirements of phase I of QFD. *Robustness, cost, design for manufacture (DFM),* and *complexity* are good candidates for any Pugh analysis.
3. The team members discuss, merge, and prioritize the criteria on their lists, usually reducing the lists to fewer than 20 criteria. Also, at the beginning of the first working session, they also discuss the criteria, to better understand them.
4. The team chooses one of the design alternatives as the baseline (datum). Note: This is best done in the early stages, frequently completed with detailed sketches.
5. The team sets up a matrix with the criteria down the left side and concepts across the top.
6. The team members rate each design alternative by each of the requirement criteria relative to the baseline (datum), using the following scale:

   + clearly better than the baseline
   s about the same as the baseline
   - clearly worse than the baseline

   Note: As the team completes its comparison, disagreements may arise stemming from different interpretations of the selection criteria. If this happens, clarify the item and begin again. For each cell of the matrix, the team must really know whether each alternative is better than, worse than, or the same as the datum. (It may need to use DOE or FMEA.)

7. After all comparisons are completed, the team totals the +'s and -'s for each alternative.

8. The team will then usually choose to focus on the alternative with the most pluses and fewest minuses. However, instead of simply selecting this alternative, the team may work at removing the minuses by examining alternatives that do better by the criterion in question. Through the concept selection process, the team may be able to *create an alternative* that is *superior* to any initially used in the comparison. The scores can be used to rank the concepts and help the team make decisions—to continue considering, to drop from consideration, to revise, or to combine with other concept(s). This process is repeated until an alternative wins out; it may take several sessions.

Concepts						
Criteria	**A**	**B**	**C**	**D**	**E**	**F**
Ease of use	0	–	0	–	–	0
Ease of transport	0	–	–	0	+	0
Reliability	+	+	0	+	0	+
Accuracy	0	0	0	0	–	0
Durability	0	0	0	0	0	+
Aesthetics	+	–	–	0	–	0
Sum of +	2	1	0	1	1	2
Sum of 0	5	2	5	4	2	4
Sum of –	0	3	2	1	3	0
Score of	2	–2	–2	0	–2	2
Rank	1	3	3	2	3	1
Continue	Yes	No	No	Yes	No	Yes

Figure 7-3. Pugh matrix

There are variations on scoring. For greater discrimination among choices, for example, the team could use a seven-level scale:

+3 meets criterion far better than baseline
+2 meets criterion much better than baseline
+1 meets criterion better than baseline
 0 meets criterion as well as baseline
-1 meets criterion not as well as baseline
-2 meets criterion much worse than baseline
-3 meets criterion far worse than baseline

The scores should be used for guidance in making decisions, not treated as absolutes. If the two top scores are very similar, then the team should examine the concepts more closely. If it's impossible to make a comparison, the team should get more information on the concepts.

Design for X (DFx)

Traditionally, design starts with sketches of parts and assemblies. These sketches are then passed to the manufacturing and assembly engineers, who are responsible for optimizing the processes used to produce the final product. Frequently, manufacturing and assembly problems are discovered at this stage and requests for changes are made. The later in the development cycle the change occurs, the more expensive the change becomes. That's why DFx is such an important part of DFSS, both in the Identify phase, to select a product concept, and in the Design phase, to assess and manage risks. These early design reviews improve quality, lower costs, and reduce time to market.

Design for X is the value-added service of using best practices in the design stage to improve X, where X is one of a proliferation of purposes or concerns. Here are many of the members of the growing DFx family now in use:

• DFM—Design for Manufacturability/Manufacture/
  Manufacturing

- DFA—Design for Assembly
- DFMA—Design for Manufacturability/Manufacture/ Manufacturing and Assembly
- DFR—Design for Reliability
- DFT—Design for Testability/Testing
- DFC—Design for Cost
- DFS—Design for Serviceability/Service
- DFQ—Design for Quality
- DFF—Design for Fabrication
- DFD—Design for Disassembly
- DFD—Design for Diagnosis
- DFI—Design for Inspection/Design for International
- DFG—Design for Green

Design for Manufacture (DFM) is a methodology for designing product components in a way that facilitates their fabrication.

Design for Assembly (DFA) simplifies the product structure, reduces the number of parts, and thereby reduces the total cost of parts. Thus, DFA reduces not only assembly costs, but also manufacturing costs.

Design for Manufacture and Assembly (DFMA)® (Boothroyd Dewhurst, Inc.) combines DFM and DFA, of course, to design products to optimize the relationship between design function, manufacturability, and ease of assembly. This helps reduce manufacturing cycle time and ultimately the cost of manufacture. DFMA requires a collaboration between all engineers, beginning with product conception all the way through to delivery.

> **DFMA Cuts Parts, Time, and Costs**
>
> Ingersoll-Rand successfully used DFMA to reduce the product development time of a portable compressor from two years to one. Moreover, the design team was able to reduce the number of parts in the product's radiator and oil cooler from 80 to 29, the number of fasteners from 38 to 20, and the time for total assembly from 18.5 minutes to 6.5 minutes.

Design for Reliability (DFR) is one of the most critical elements of DFSS. Reliability is the ability of a product to satisfactorily perform its designated function over its customer intended lifetime. It has been referred to as "quality over time" and is a major bottom-line assessment of product performance in customers' minds, especially at the time of repurchase.

Design for Testability (DFT) encourages the early involvement of test engineering or quality assurance functions in the design process. This can minimize the cost of developing or acquiring new equipment as well as the cost of testing the product at each stage of production. Where production volumes are high, automated test equipment may be cost-effective. Testing equipment and procedures at the same time the product is being designed can reduce lead time. Designing products to use standardized equipment can further reduce the costs of test equipment and reduce the lead time for testing.

Design for Cost (DFC) is an approach with a narrow, obvious focus that uses such product design tools as Quality Function Deployment, Design for Manufacturing and Assembly, and Value Analysis/Function Analysis.

Design for Serviceability/Service (DFS) involves paying attention to the serviceability or maintenance of products early in the design process. Those responsible for product maintenance and service need to be consulted early on to share their concerns and requirements. Designing support processes should be done parallel to the design of the product. This can result in lower life cycle costs and a product design that considers serviceability.

With high-reliability, low-cost, or consumable products, maintenance is less important than with products that have a long life cycle or with products that have parts that are subject to wear. For these products, the following design rules can be helpful:

- Use unique connectors with electrical parts, to avoid misconnections.
- Identify parts that are subject to wear. Design these parts so

that they can be accessed, removed, and replaced easily.
- Use common hand tools and a minimum of hand tools for assembly and disassembly.
- Place the items most likely to fail, wear out, or need replacement in a small number of modules or assemblies.
- Eliminate or reduce the need for adjustment.
- Employ quick fastening and unfastening mechanisms for serviceable parts.
- Use standard replacement parts.

Design for International (DFI) means designing products that are suitable for worldwide distribution. This means designing products that can be quickly adapted to each country or market. This requires attention to varying standards, differing power requirements, differing safety and environmental standards, and differences in language and culture.

Design for Green (DFG) or Design for Environment (DFE) shows concern for producing in environmentally conscious ways. With environmental regulations increasing and concern for the environment growing, manufacturers are reevaluating their manufacturing processes to minimize the impact on our environment.

Manager's Checklist for Chapter 7

❑ It's important to set up for each phase of a DFSS project a phase-gate review, during which a multi-functional management team reviews and assesses the project according to the plan set forth in the project charter.

❑ Benchmarking in DFSS can be part of selecting a project and also a means of eliminating potential failure modes from the design.

❑ When the project team identifies channels for process capability data, it should conduct a measurement system analysis. This generally involves six factors: repeatability, reproducibility, stability, linearity, bias, and discrimination.

❏ DFSS focuses on determining what customers require and value, through a range of tools, including customer survey analysis, affinity diagramming, quality function deployment (QFD) and the house of quality, the Kano model, the voice of the customer table, and analytic hierarchy process.

❏ DFSS scorecards provide a systematic way for the project team to set goals, predict results, calculate capability, identify gaps, and track performance as progress toward the goals.

❏ For evaluating design alternatives, a project team can use the Pugh concept selection technique and the failure modes and affects analysis (FMEA).

❏ A project team can use any of a family of design reviews known as Design for X (DFx) to select a product concept and to assess and manage risks. These early design reviews improve quality, lower costs, and reduce time to market.

DFSS Tools, Part 2

This chapter concludes our brief look at the tools more commonly used in Design for Six Sigma.

Failure Modes and Effects Analysis (FMEA)

Perhaps the first thing to mention about this DFSS tool is the least important—the name. It began as Failure Modes and Effects Criticality Analysis (FMECA), but is generally now FMEA—although that acronym may stand for Failure Mode (singular) and Effect (singular) Analysis, Failure Mode (singular) and Effects (plural) Analysis, or Failure Modes (plural) and Effects (plural) Analysis.

We mentioned FMEA in Chapter 7 as a means of prioritizing customer requirements. The project team can use it in evaluating a design concept for potential failure modes so it can address them early in the design effort. FMEA provides an excellent basis for classifying characteristics, for identifying CTQs and other critical variables. One objective of FMEA is to

> **Failure modes and effects analysis (FMEA)** A system-atic group of activities intended to recognize and evaluate the potential failure of a product or process and its effects, identify actions that could eliminate or reduce the chance of the potential failure occurring, and document the process. This tool is used in the early conception phase of products and processes to help iden-tify and counter weak points. FMEA can be combined with decision analysis methods such as the analytic hierarchy process (AHP) and quality function deployment (QFD) to help plan for preventive actions. Also known as *failure mode and effect analysis, failure mode and effects analysis,* and *failure mode, effects, and criticality analysis.* Too often design teams complete FMEA after the design is completed, which reduces this technique to being little more than a paperwork exercise. For maximum benefit, FMEA must be a proactive activity, completed in conjunction with the design.

direct the available resources toward the most promising oppor-tunities. It's also used to define special considerations for testing and other activities to minimize failure risk. FMEA can be used in conjunction with concept selection, detailed design activities, and process design.

But FMEA is more often used in the Verify phase and the Control phase, to assess risk and to recommend corrective actions. In fact, the project team should always do an FMEA whenever a product failure would mean potential harm or dam-age for the user of the product.

Basics

To execute FMEA properly, assemble the right team:

- people who know the intimate details of the design or process
- representatives of the customers' viewpoint
- representatives of other affected areas
- an FMEA facilitator
- a project manager who will ensure follow-up and account-ability

Then, follow these basic steps:

1. Define the system to be analyzed. Agree on the level of FMEA and delimit the scope; too much detail can be impractical. Identify both internal and interface functions, the performance expected at all system levels, and system restraints. Define every type of failure and each goal in terms of functions and conditions.
2. Build process maps that show the operations and interrelationships of functional entities.
3. Do a SIPOC (Supplier, Input, Process, Output, Customer) analysis for each process in the system.
4. List the intended function of each step in every process.
5. Identify every potential failure mode for each process step and define the effects, both immediate and eventual.
6. Evaluate each failure mode in terms of the worst potential results and rate it from 1 to 10 for severity (SEV).
7. Evaluate each failure mode in terms of the likelihood of occurring and rate it from 1 to 10 for occurrence (OCC).
8. Evaluate each failure mode in terms of the detection methods and rate it from 1 to 10 for detectability (DET).
9. Multiply the SEV rating by the OCC rating by the DET rating to calculate the risk priority number (RPN) for the system. The RPN is useful in setting priorities for correction and compensation.
10. Determine provisions to correct the design or to compensate for each failure mode, in order to eliminate failure or control the risk.
11. Identify for any corrective actions the effects on the system.
12. Rate severity, occurrence, and detectability after all corrective actions and calculate the new RPN.
13. Document the FMEA and summarize any problems that could not be corrected and identify any special controls necessary to reduce the risk of failure.

Variants

There are several variants of FMEA, to serve more specific purposes. They include the following:

FMEA Ratings: Questions and Extremes
Severity (SEV)
How significant would the effect of this failure be to the customer?
Rating (extremes):
1—The effect would be of minor significance: the customer would not notice it or would consider it insignificant.
10—The effect would be disastrous: it would endanger the customer and/or violate laws or regulations.
Occurrence (OCC)
How likely is it that the cause of this failure would occur?
Rating (extremes):
1—The cause of this failure is unlikely to occur.
10—This failure occurs nearly all the time.
Detectability (DET)
How likely is it that the system would detect the failure?
Rating (extremes):
1—The system is almost certain to detect the failure before it reaches the customer.
10—The system is almost certain to not detect the failure before it reaches the customer.

- design failure mode(s) and effects analysis (DFMEA): focuses on components and subsystems
- process failure mode(s) and effects analysis (PFMEA): focuses on manufacturing and assembly processes
- system failure mode(s) and effects analysis (SFMEA): focuses on global system functions
- software failure mode(s) and effects analysis (SFMEA): focuses on software functions
- service failure mode(s) and effects analysis (SFMEA): focuses on service functions
- damage mode(s) and effects analysis (DMEA): uses results of FMEA and provides early criteria for damage or vulnerability assessment

Anticipatory Failure Determination (AFD)

Anticipatory Failure Determination® (a trademark of Ideation International) is a failure analysis method. It can be used to analyze earlier failures, but in DFSS it's used, like FMEA, to identify and minimize potential failures, both in the design of the product and in the design of the process. But, unlike FMEA, which is used to look for a cause of a failure mode, Anticipatory Failure Determination (AFD) is used to reverse the problem and view a failure as something intended—and the project team tries to devise ways to ensure that the failure always happens reliably.

AFD offers an advantage over FMEA for more complex failure analysis. FMEA works because team members identify failures and their root causes through personal experience or the knowledge of others. But there can be a complication here: people tend to resist thinking about unpleasant possibilities unless they've experienced them—and even then they may be reluctant to identify or document those problems. AFD, by reversing the problem, overcomes this psychological issue and opens up the analysis of failures.

AFD consists of the following steps:

- Formulate the problem. Describe the failure.
- Formulate the problem in reverse. Describe how to make the failure occur.
- Identify the conditions leading to the failure. Determine the events involved in the failure and localize it.
- Search for ways to produce the failure. Identify anything that could lead to the failure.
- Make sure that the resources needed to cause the failure are available for each of the potential solutions.

This reversal of thinking seems simple, but it has great advantages, according to Jack Hipple, principal in Innovation-TRIZ, Inc.:

The psychological effect of switching the question from "What could go wrong?" to "How can I make it go wrong?" is simply amazing .... Our brains go into a different quadrant and will identify many ways to sabotage a system or cause it to fail than *any* checklist process you are currently using. The process is especially powerful when the participants have expert knowledge. These inside experts would *know exactly how to make it fail*, but just don't think that way.

Poka-Yoke

Poka-Yoke is a mistake-proofing methodology developed by a Japanese manufacturing engineer, Shigeo Shingo of Toyota, in the 1960s. Poka-Yoke (pronounced "poh-kah yoh-kay") translates into English as "to avoid" (yokeru) "inadvertent error" (poka).

Poka-Yoke for assembly means designs that will not allow improper assembly. Poka-Yoke in processes means designing the process, equipment, and tools to prevent errors by ensuring that an operation cannot be performed incorrectly. Poka-Yoke is also useful in non-manufacturing businesses. A Poka-

A Switch to Error-Proofing

Shingo made a lot of Poka-Yoke believers at the Yamada Electric plant in 1961. The factory was having a problem with one of its products, with a small switch that contained two push buttons supported by two springs. Sometimes, workers assembling the switch would forget to insert a spring. Occasionally a defective unit would be shipped to a customer; then the factory would dispatch an engineer to disassemble the switch, insert the missing spring, and reassemble the switch. That little problem was both costly and embarrassing and—despite renewed vigilance—management was unable to prevent it.

Shingo came up with a solution that became the first Poka-Yoke device. He added a step to the assembly process. Instead of taking two springs out of a large box of parts and assembling the switch, the worker would now first take two springs out of the parts box and place them on a small dish placed in front of the box and then assemble the switch. The new method made it obvious if the worker forgot to insert a spring. That simple change completely solved the problem.

Yoke device is one that prevents incorrect parts from being made or assembled or that easily identifies a flaw or error.

Poka-Yoke is one of the main components of Shingo's Zero Quality Control (ZQC) system, which intends to produce zero defective products. One means is through Poka-Yoke, small devices that are used to either detect errors or prevent them.

Shingo has worked on developing the concept of Poka-Yoke for the past three decades. One important distinction he made was between a *mistake* and a *defect*. Mistakes are inevitable; people cannot be expected to concentrate on their work 100% of the time or to completely understand their instructions. Defects result when a mistake is allowed to reach a customer, and defects are avoidable. The goal of Poka-Yoke is to engineer the process in order to either prevent mistakes or immediately detect and correct them.

Good Poka-Yoke devices share the following characteristics:

- They are simple and cheap. If they are too complicated or expensive, they will not be cost-effective.
- They are part of the process and receive immediate inspection.
- They are placed close to where mistakes occur, providing quick feedback to workers so mistakes can be corrected.

Process Capability and Performance Studies

Process capability, as defined in Chapter 3, is a statistical measure of inherent variation for a given event in a stable process. In other words, it's the ability of a process to produce outputs that meet requirements. Another way of looking at process capability is that it's the range over which the natural variation of a process occurs as determined by the system of common causes.

Process capability studies are designed to yield specific information about the performance of a process under specified operating conditions. A process capability study is a preliminary statistical study of process output, on a limited population. It uses the process variability and the process specifications to

Process capability The six sigma range of common cause variation for processes that are statistically stable. Process capability indices usually use *estimated sigma*.

Estimated sigma An estimate of the standard deviation calculated by dividing the average range by the tabular constant d2 (R-bar/d2).

Capability index A mathematical calculation that predicts the probability of process output to conform to specifications. More specifically, it's a ratio of the specification width to the natural tolerance of the process. A capability index has meaning only for a process exhibiting statistical control, a process that is stable, in which variations in the sampling results can be attributed to a constant system of *common causes*, as opposed to *special causes*—variables that are not a part of the process. In other words, when a process is under statistical control, results are predictable, so a capability index has meaning.

predict the quality level (i.e., reject rate) that can be expected from that process. The objective is to identify and eliminate sources of process variation in order to minimize the reject rate.

Capability indices are mathematical calculations that predict the probability of process output to conform to specifications. Capability indices have meaning only for processes that exhibit statistical control, because a process will yield results that are predictable only when the levels of variability are stable.

Process capability is understood, measured, and indicated in three ways—Cp, Cpk, and Cr.

The Cpk capability index tells how well a process can meet specification limits. It's calculated using estimated sigma, so it shows the potential to meet specifications. Since this calculation takes into account the location of the process average, the process does not need to be centered on the target value. The higher the Cpk, the less variation between the process output and specifications. If the Cpk is 1.0, 99.73% of the outputs are within the specifications. If the Cpk is between 0 and 1.0, not all of the output is meeting the specifications.

The Cp capability index tells how well a process can meet upper and lower specification limits. Like the Cpk, it uses estimated sigma, so it shows the *potential* to meet specifications.

However, the Cp ignores the process average; it's a measure of spread only. The higher the Cp, the

> **Spread** the range of data from the lowest value to the highest value.

smaller the spread of the output. If the system is not centered within the specifications, the Cp alone may be misleading. A process with a high Cp (a narrow spread) may not meet customer needs if it's not centered within the specifications.

The Cr capability ratio summarizes the estimated spread of the system in comparison with the spread of the upper and lower specification limits. The lower the Cr, the smaller the output spread. Cr does not consider process centering. When the Cr is multiplied by 100, the result shows the percent of the specifications that are being used by the variation in the process. Cr is calculated using an estimated sigma. Cr is the reciprocal of Cp; in other words, Cr = 1 / Cp.

The smaller the difference between the Cpk and the Cp, the more centered the process is. If the process is centered on its target value, the Cpk and Cp will be equal.

Process Performance

Process performance is defined as the extent to which a process meets its performance criteria and, more technically, as the six sigma range of inherent variation for processes that are statistically stable.

Process capability is understood, measured, and indicated in three ways—Pp, Ppk, and Pr.

The Ppk performance index tells how well a system is meeting the specifications. Ppk calculations use actual sigma (sigma of the individuals), so Ppk shows how the process

> **Process performance** The six sigma range of inherent variation for processes that are statistically stable. Process performance indices usually use *sigma of the individuals*.
>
> **Sigma of the individuals** Standard deviation calculated from the individual values in a set of data, also known as *actual sigma* or *calculated sigma*.

is actually running in terms of the specifications. This index also takes into account how well the process is centered within the specification limits. The higher the Ppk, the less variation between process output and the specifications. If the Ppk is 1.0, 99.73% of the outputs are within specifications. If the Ppk is between 0 and 1.0, not all process output is meeting the specifications.

The Pp performance index summarizes the performance of a process in terms of meeting upper and lower specification limits. The Pp, like the Ppk, uses actual sigma (sigma of the individuals), so it shows how the system is actually running in terms of the specifications. However, it ignores the process average; the Pp is a measure of spread only. The higher the Pp, the smaller the spread of the system's output. If the system is not centered within the specifications, Pp alone may be misleading. A process with a high Pp (a narrow spread) may not meet customer needs if it's not centered within the specifications.

The Pr performance ratio summarizes the spread of the process in comparison with the spread of the upper and lower specification limits. The lower the Pr, the smaller the output spread. Pr does not consider process centering. When the Pr value is multiplied by 100, the result is the percent of the specifications that are being used by the variation in the process. Pr is calculated using the actual sigma (sigma of the individuals). Pr is the reciprocal of Pp; in other words, $Pr = 1 / Pp$.

The Pp and the Ppk should be used together to account for both spread and centering. The smaller the difference between the Ppk and the Pp, the more centered the process is. When the process is centered on its target value, the Ppk and the Pp will be equal.

Multi-Vari Analysis

Multi-vari analysis is used to identify significant factors that cause process variation. In a multi-vari study, a process is monitored as it runs in its normal state and analyzed to determine relationships between key process input variables (KPIVs) and key process output variables (KPOVs). By noting the state of KPIVs and the simultaneous state of KPOVs, the project team may be able to find useful correlations.

There are three basic steps in a multi-vari study.

1. Identify sources of variation. There are three families of variations:
   - positional—variation within a specific product, due to a similar process across a production line (e.g., among machines, among operators)
   - cyclical: variation among products in a sequence or across a series of processes (e.g., between consecutive pieces or services, from batch to batch)
   - temporal: variation in a process over time (e.g., from shift to shift, from setup to setup, from week to week)
2. Sample the families. Use sampling to measure variability. There are several types of representative sampling:
   - random sampling—check sample parts or units at random (using random number tables)
   - systematic sampling—check every Nth part or unit
   - subgroup sampling—check the output of a step or an activity at a specified frequency (e.g., check 10 units at 7:00 a.m., at 11:00 a.m., at 3:00 p.m., at 7:00 p.m.)
   - cluster or stratified sampling—check random parts or units within each of a set of groups (e.g., check random credit purchases from customers in five age groups: under 25, 26-35, 36-45, and over 46)
3. Use graphical analysis. Graph the results, using a multi-vari plot, a box plot, a main effects plot, or a regression plot.

Sometimes multi-vari analysis will reveal the sources of problems. In other cases, the outputs of a multi-vari analysis can become the inputs to a designed experiment (DOE).

Design of Experiments (DOE)

To develop and optimize products and processes, a project team needs to identify cause-and-effect relationships. Sometimes, there may be many potential causes or the effects may be complicated by variation. That's when Design of Experiments is so powerful.

This is the most effective method for solving complex problems with many variables. It may be used in producing robust product designs or in determining optimal process control settings.

The traditional experimental design, changing only one factor for each run and holding the others constant as a control, requires many runs—one for each possible value for each factor. Also, it doesn't reveal interactions between variables. To counter these two disadvantages, the DOE methods were developed in the early 20th century in England by an agricultural scientist, Ronald Fisher, for studying the effects of various treatments, such as soil conditions and fertilizers, upon crop yields.

DOE uses statistics to allow the project team to run the minimum number of experiments to optimize the product or process design. It involves determining the best experiments to run to fit a particular mathematical model. It's an efficient, reliable method for determining cause and effect relationships among multiple factors (inputs) and response variables (effects).

The team starts by identifying the input variables and the output response(s) to be measured. For each input variable, the team defines a number of levels that represent the range for which they want to know the effect of that variable. An experimental plan is produced that tells where to set each test parameter for each run of the test. Then, the response is measured for each run. Any differences in outputs among the groups of inputs are then attributed to *single effects*—input variables acting alone—or *interactions*—input variables acting in combination.

The most common DOE method is to select an orthogonal array—a matrix of numbers in rows and columns—to experiment over a wide variety of factor settings, while keeping the effects of each factor separate. Each row represents the state of the factors in a given experiment and each column represents a specific factor that can be changed between experimental runs. (The array is called "orthogonal" because each of the effects of the various factors can be separated from the others.) At its simplest, the orthogonal arrays can be solved as a series of simultaneous equations. With more complex, partially orthogonal designs, advanced statistical techniques, such as regression analysis, are used. (This is a good job for software—and a bad job for humans!)

In order to derive complete information regarding all factor effects and interactions, the matrix must contain all possible combinations of factors and levels. Unfortunately this almost always requires too many experimental runs to be practical. In most industrial environments, at least the higher-order interaction effects can be safely ignored, allowing for the use of fractional factorial designs, which require far fewer runs.

The following are the basic steps in a designed experiment:

- Identify the factors to be evaluated.
- Define the levels of the factors to be tested.
- Create an array of experimental combinations.
- Conduct the experiment under prescribed conditions.
- Evaluate the results and conclusions.

DOE, if used judiciously, helps to identify the key attributes and shorten design development time. A DOE analysis can achieve several objectives. First, it can provide crucial insights into the operating levels to use to create a robust design, a product or process design that's essentially insensitive to conditions of use (for products) or operation (for processes). Second, it identifies which experimental factors are so influential on the key performance metrics that they require constant monitoring (through SPC or other means). Third, it can be used for general mathematical models that can be used as transfer functions.

To show how DOE works, very simplistically, let's take a

simple example. We're designing a widget and considering five factors, each of which could have either of two values.

One design for the experiment would be to run all possible combinations of factors. This is called a *full factorial* experiment. As there are five factors at two levels each, our experiment would require 32 runs (2 x 2 x 2 x 2 x 2 or 2^5).

We could also use orthogonal designs requiring 8, 12, or 16 runs. These are commonly called *fractional* or *fractional factorial* experiments. Each of these three designs would cover the experimental region of the five factors and two values and each would have advantages and disadvantages.

Fractional experiments allow investigation of the main effects and/or lower-order interactions of factors without the time and expense of running full factorial experiments. A *half-fraction* experiment would involve half the treatment combinations required by a full factorial—our 16 runs in this example. A *quarter-fraction* experiment would involve one-fourth the treatment combinations required by a full factorial—eight runs for our widget design.

It's essential to verify the results of any experiment. Experimenters typically verify (at a minimum) the best predicted results from the experiment.

Response Surface Methodology (RSM)

The statistical experiment designs most widely used in optimization experiments are termed *response surface designs*. As defined in Chapter 3, a response surface is a surface that represents predicted responses to variations in factors. A surface can have any number of dimensions, depending on the number of factors.

Response surface methodology (RSM), which derives its name from the use of these widely used optimization experiment designs, is one approach to product and process optimization work. It's typically a second phase in experimental design and is critical in optimizing process performance, generally used after a set of designed experiments have screened out the less important factors.

The primary purpose of RSM is to determine the optimal settings for the factors that influence the response. Response surface designs contain trials in which the variables are set at extreme levels. They may also contain trials in which one or more of the variables is set at the midpoint of the study range and may be set at other levels within the range. Thus, these designs provide information on direct effects, pairwise interaction effects, and curvilinear variable effects.

As defined in Chapter 3, RSM is a statistical technique that uses response surfaces to analyze quantitative data from experiments to determine and simultaneously solve multivariant equations.

Response surface methods can be used to answer a number of questions:

1. How do a set of variables affect a particular response over a specified region?
2. What settings of the variables will result in a product or process that meets specifications?
3. What settings of the variables will yield a maximum (or minimum) response and what is the local geography of the response surface(s) near these maximal (minimal) values?

The application of RSM to design optimization is an effective means of minimizing the cost and time associated with traditional experimental approaches.

Monte Carlo Simulation

Process simulation uses a computerized model that approximates the operation of a process, using the critical operating parameters of the real process. A process model allows the project team to simulate a process far more rapidly than would be possible in reality and collect large samples of data to analyze.

Some simulation packages use an analysis method called Monte Carlo simulation. Monte Carlo analysis is the repeated

> **Key Term**
>
> **Monte Carlo simulation** A statistical method of analysis that estimates possible outcomes from a set of random variables by simulating a process a large number of times and observing the outcomes, which represent a distribution of likely results.

observation of a simulation of the system, using inputs randomly varying within an assumed distribution.

With this method, each consecutive run of a simulation uses a combination of input values taken at random from selected input parameters. Since the program can simulate a process operation in a minimum of time, the project team can collect a plethora of data in minutes. If configured properly, this high-speed simulation provides long-term data rather than only the short-term data that the real process operation would produce (from pilot builds), so the team may have a clearer picture of how the process performance will vary over the long term.

Robust Design: Taguchi Methods

Taguchi methods is a generic term covering a variety of practices developed by Genichi Taguchi for statistically determining required quantitative features of a design that make it robust against disturbances, variations, and uncertainties, with the objective of reducing loss to society.

Robustness, as defined by Taguchi, describes the state in which the performance of a product or a process is minimally sensitive to factors causing variability (either in the manufacturing or use environment) and aging at the lowest manufacturing cost. Developing a *robust design* means optimizing the settings of controllable factors that will make a product or process insensitive to variation in factors that are uncontrollable or that we choose not to control.

The methods consider the noise factors—variation in manufacturing, environmental variation during use of the product, and deterioration of component—and the cost of failure in the field in order to help ensure customer satisfaction. Taguchi methods focus on designing efficient experiments, increasing signal-to-noise

> **Robustness** The state in which the performance of a product or a process is minimally sensitive to factors causing variability (either in the manufacturing or use environment) and aging at the lowest manufacturing cost.

ratios, and building in tolerances to allow for manufacturing variables known to be avoidable. These methods are considered by advocates of the Taguchi approach to be the most powerful of optimization methods.

Traditional engineering focuses on testing one factor at a time or selecting test combinations based upon technical knowledge. In contrast, robust design allows design teams to perform experiments and test prototypes on multiple factors at once, so it's an efficient, cost-effective way to improve the design of products and processes.

Robust design strategy uses five primary tools:

1. *P-diagram*, for classifying the variables associated with the product into four types—signal (input), response (output), noise, and control.
2. *Ideal function*, for identifying the ideal relationship between the signal and the response.
3. *Quadratic loss function* (or *quality loss function*), for quantifying the loss due to deviation from target performance.
4. *Signal-to-noise ratio*, for predicting field quality through laboratory experiments.
5. *Orthogonal arrays,* for gathering dependable information about control factors (design parameters) with a small number of experiments (as discussed above with Design of Experiments).

Tolerancing and Tolerance Analysis

A tolerance is an acceptability limit. Tolerance is a specification of what's acceptable (within tolerance) and what's unacceptable (outside tolerance). If a part dimension could be measured as 23.00 ± 0.20 mm, this specification contains a target value of 23.00 and a tolerance of 0.20. This would mean that any part measuring between 22.80 mm and 23.20 mm would be

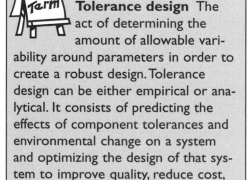

Tolerance An acceptable range of variation, usually defined by the maximum and minimum limit values for the dimensions of a product to meet customer requirements. Tolerance is a specification of what's acceptable (within tolerance) and what's unacceptable (outside tolerance).

acceptable and that any part smaller than 22.80 mm or larger than 23.20 mm would be unacceptable.

Tolerance design is the act of determining the amount of allowable variability around parameters in order to create a robust design. Tolerance design can be either empirical or analytical. It consists of two main activities:

- Predict the effects of component tolerances and environmental change on a system.
- Optimize the design of that system to improve quality, reduce cost, and minimize time to market.

Tolerance design The act of determining the amount of allowable variability around parameters in order to create a robust design. Tolerance design can be either empirical or analytical. It consists of predicting the effects of component tolerances and environmental change on a system and optimizing the design of that system to improve quality, reduce cost, and minimize time to market.

Control Plan

No Design for Six Sigma project is complete without a control plan. It ensures that the quality designed into the product, the service, or the process will remain. A control plan answers three questions:

- What have we done to prevent defects?
- How will we know if defects occur?
- What will we do if defects occur?

A control plan is a written description of the system(s) for controlling parts, assemblies, products, and processes, to address the important characteristics and requirements of the design. Each part or assembly should have a control plan, although one control plan can cover more than one part if produced through a common process. Failure Modes and Effects Analysis (FMEA), which was used earlier in the DFSS process to identify potential problems, is used at this point to help direct the development of control plans to *prevent* problems.

> **Control plan** A written description of the system(s) for controlling parts, assemblies, products, and processes, to address the important characteristics and requirements of the design.
>
> **Control chart** A tool for monitoring changes in a process, by distinguishing between variations that are inherent in the process (common cause) and variations that result in a change (special cause).

The purpose of a process control plan is to enable monitoring of the design characteristics and associated process variables to ensure capability and stability of the product or process over time. Every DFSS project should include a control plan and a control chart (if applicable).

A control plan describes the actions required at each step in the process. During product development, the project team uses the control plan to document and communicate the initial plan for process control and updates the control plan as the design changes. During production, the control plan guides manufacturing in order to monitor and control the process and ensure product quality.

Tools, Tools, and More Tools

As mentioned at the start of Chapter 7, a book of this scope cannot present all of the DFSS tools—and none of them in sufficient detail. That's why we recommend making the most of your MBB and BBs and reading *The Six Sigma Handbook* (New York: McGraw-Hill, 2000) and *The Six Sigma Project Planner* (New York: McGraw-Hill, 2003) by Thomas Pyzdek and *Design for Six Sigma in Technology and Product Development* by Clyde M. Creveling, Jeffrey Lee Slutsky, and David Antis Jr. (Upper Saddle River NJ: Prentice Hall, 2002).

Manager's Checklist for Chapter 8

❏ The project team can use Failure Modes and Effects Analysis in evaluating a design concept for potential failure modes so it can address them early in the design effort. FMEA provides an excellent basis for classifying characteristics, for identifying CTQs and other critical variables.

❏ Anticipatory Failure Determination is a failure analysis method that can be used in DFSS to identify and minimize potential failures. AFD is used to reverse the problem and view a failure as something intended—and the project team tries to devise ways to ensure that the failure always happens reliably.

❏ Poka-Yoke is a mistake-proofing methodology that will not allow errors.

❏ The project team conducts process capability studies to obtain specific information about the performance of a process under specified operating conditions, in order to identify and eliminate sources of process variation, and conducts process performance studies to measure the extent to which a process meets its performance criteria.

❏ Multi-vari analysis is used to identify significant factors that cause process variation.

❏ Design of Experiments (DOE) is the most effective method for solving complex problems with many variables. It may be used in producing robust product designs or in determining optimal process control settings.

❏ Response surface methodology (RSM) is a second phase in experimental design and critical in optimizing process performance, generally used after a set of designed experiments have screened out the less important factors.

❏ Process simulation creates a computerized model that approximates the operation of a process. Monte Carlo simulation estimates possible outcomes by simulating a process a large number of times and observing the outcomes.

❏ Taguchi methods is a generic term covering a variety of practices for determining required quantitative features of a design that make it robust against disturbances, variations, and uncertainties, in order to reduce loss of quality.

❏ Tolerance design consists of predicting the effects of component tolerances and environmental change on a system and optimizing the design of that system to improve quality, reduce cost, and minimize time to market.

❏ No Design for Six Sigma project is complete without a control plan. It ensures that the quality designed into the product, the service, or the process will remain.

How to Sustain Design for Six Sigma

Six Sigma is a methodology that needs to continue indefinitely, because there's always room for improving designs and processes. So how do you do it? That's the focus of this chapter.

After 99.99966%, What Next?

OK, so let's imagine that your DFSS projects have achieved their goals and that you're offering products and services that are at a six sigma level, with processes that are also at that ideal of 99.99966%. What next?

All of the successes of Six Sigma and Design for Six Sigma and all of the emphasis on six sigma levels of quality and customer satisfaction may make some managers confident about the future and complacent. After all, you've first improved through using Six Sigma and then you've Designed for Six Sigma, so you should have great competitive advantages, right? Absolutely! This would be a tremendous accomplishment and you need to celebrate this accomplishment. But you must not let complacency set in around the organization.

We need only think back to Chapter 4 and the 1.5 sigma shift—or, more properly, the *long-term dynamic mean variation*. This shift of the process average, the degradation from the short-term capability to the long-term performance, seems inevitable.

As we mentioned in Chapter 4, what this means, in simple terms, is that the performance of the product, service, or process that a project team designs to meet the rigorous six sigma level will decline over time. Small declines will likely not prevent your products from meeting a high level of acceptability, but that may generally not be good enough—especially after you've set your goal as six sigma and achieved it.

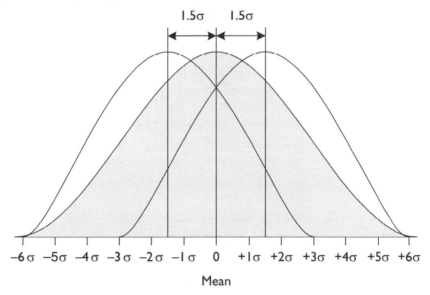

Figure 9-1. Sigma shift

So this chapter is about how to fight complacency, how to build upon the initial results of DFSS, and how to spread DFSS throughout the organization ... and beyond.

It's important to recognize that there's no room for complacency or easing off on DFSS projects—sustaining their gains is critical to the continual success of your initiative. All of the steps listed point in one direction: keep it focused, moving forward, and in the forefront of everything you do.

Keeping the Capability

The first and best means of sustaining the gains achieved through DFSS is Six Sigma: use it diligently to improve the processes designed through DFSS. In other words, do what it takes to maintain the capability of the design.

When the design of a product, a service, or a process has achieved the goals set for it, the project team establishes control measures to sustain that high level of performance. Then, the process owner should monitor performance and communicate the results. If necessary, a Six Sigma team can be formed to improve the product, service, or process, to continue the success that was built into the design.

What capability does your target process demonstrate in terms of your metrics? What are the factors affecting that capability? How do you keep and control it?

Once you know that, you can work to maintain the optimum and consistent performance of the process. Whether you're producing goods or providing services, once you know what you can achieve, you can retain it for sustained productivity and profitability.

Keep the Customers in Mind and Involved

Paying attention to the voice of the customer doesn't end when the design is developed and optimized. Rather, continue to focus on the customers. Keep getting input, using means such as those cited in Chapter 3:

- customer complaints: encourage them and review them regularly
- surveys: target specifically the new product or service
- focus groups: arrange sessions to discuss the new product or service
- one-on-one interviews: find out what individuals think

- contextual inquiry: test the product or service with customers

Find better ways to get input. Finally, find ways to discover the customer's latent needs and expectations.

Make the Most of What You Know

It's possible to contribute to sustaining the gains obtained through DFSS by knowledge transfer. It's important to provide coaching and training to ensure that the members of the project team transfer their knowledge to others and share information throughout the DFSS phases.

The difficult process of managing information during Six Sigma projects can be made easier through Web-based software applications that maximize knowledge transfer and access for all members of the design project team.

Not all knowledge transfer requires technology. Since members of DFSS project team come from various areas of the organization, they can spread the word and share the knowledge more widely, taking it back home into their functions and their co-workers. Nobody keeps success a secret. Those who have learned and applied the approach and the tools are going to be sharing them.

Knowledge Management

Building and maintaining a database of "lessons learned" will allow you to document what you've learned and achieved with projects to date. That information can then be shared. Once you've fixed something, it's important to be able to share what you know about it. It's important to share the lessons throughout your organization, not only to tout your success, but to provide potential solutions for other issues elsewhere in your organization. It won't help you very much to eliminate defects and then to keep these to yourself. Knowledge transfer needs to happen continually, both inside and outside the project.

Communication

A communication plan is essential for sharing lessons learned and sustaining your Six Sigma success. Whether it's press releases, monthly newsletters, company intranet updates, video presentations, or quarterly company meetings, you need to get the message out regularly and conspicuously to people inside and outside the organization.

You can report on the progress of projects, itemize actual dollar savings to date, explain Six Sigma acronyms, or focus in on the key tools. What's essential is to keep getting the word out on the benefits of Six Sigma.

As you know, all levels of personnel should be familiar with the basics of your Six Sigma mission, including terminology, roles, and metrics. This is to ensure that people can "link" between the big picture and actionable items in their different areas. Again, it's all about communicating, in real terms, the powerful implications of each and every project.

Vision and Leadership

Leadership is required to sustain the gains of DFSS initiatives. We all know that change generally makes people uncomfortable. CEOs should expect some resistance and more than a little anxiety when implementing DFSS. If CEOs and champions do not prepare to recognize and address all of the following conditions from the beginning, any of them can impede Six Sigma initiatives:

- Senior managers are ambivalent about the initiative or even reluctant to get involved.
- Managers and employees do not understand the principles of Six Sigma and DFSS.
- Senior managers, champions, and master black belts plan initiatives that are either too broad or too narrow in scope.
- Managers and employees do not participate or even cooperate with the project teams.
- Managers fail to resolve cultural issues that stand in the way of DFSS methods and objectives.

The move to change the culture of the organization must start at the top. The CEO must provide vision and must lead the move in such a way that all of the managers accept and embrace the business imperative as a key strategy for the organization, the way of the future. Being good is not good enough. Improvements should not lead to complacency, but to greater zeal to make more improvements.

Infrastructure, Reinforcement, and Control

It's also necessary for executive management to regularly review and direct DFSS projects as it is already reviewing and directing the entire Six Sigma initiative. This ownership from the top is important to reinforce the depth and breadth of the Six Sigma commitment and to keep senior leaders involved and engaged in the process. At least quarterly, senior executives should be thoroughly informed about the progress of all current projects, the financial results achieved, and the projects ahead.

The business plan should include planning for DFSS projects. The DFSS initiative should be considered an integral element of any strategic planning. As goals are set, Six Sigma and DFSS champions, master black belts, and black belts should be involved in setting them and Six Sigma and DFSS projects should be included as key to achieving them. It's an executive responsibility to make sure that DFSS becomes inherent in all business operations and in the culture of the organization, by promoting DFSS and Six Sigma throughout the organization.

Here are some ways that leaders can structure the organization to promote and sustain DFSS:

- Build Six Sigma goals into company-wide strategic plans.
- Host quarterly reviews with senior management.
- Develop an ongoing project list that registers both projected and actual savings.
- Develop a common metric and reporting/review system that evaluates and updates the status of all projects monthly.

- Determine the next year's goals in the number of black belts, green belts, master black belts, project selection, and savings projections.

One way to ensure that you're sustaining DFSS properly is to use a "sustainability checklist," such as "The 21-Question Status Check," as a methodical approach to assessing the health of your initiative.

The 21-Question Status Check

The following 21 questions are an excellent guide to assessing the sustained performance of your Six Sigma initiative. By routinely examining and reinforcing your mission with this status check, you minimize the potential for slipping or slacking in company-wide projects. Keep asking and keep answering these fundamentally important questions and you'll keep your initiative on track:

1. Do you think the Six Sigma process is self-sustaining in your group?
2. What is the status of your master black belts?
3. What is the status of your green belts?
4. How many reviews do your senior executives attend?
5. What are the dropout rates?
6. How many projects are officially completed?
7. How many black belts are ready for certification?
8. Has the finance department been an active part of the process?
9. Have you and the finance department agreed on the guidelines that define true savings?
10. Do you currently have a manual system for tracking the backlog list of black belt projects by plant?
11. Do you have the next set of black belts identified and is upper management supportive?
12. Do you think you are focusing on implementing project completions?
13. Are you attempting to change the program or staying with the black belts' focus?
14. Should you stop doing Six Sigma?
15. What is the status report you are giving to senior management?
16. Are the controllers signing off on your projects?
17. Are the controllers aware of the savings?

18. If you were to spot-check the controllers, what defect rate would you find? (In other words, how many do not know about the savings achieved by the projects?)
19. What database are you going to use through the life of tracking your Six Sigma projects?
20. What is the status of the black belt incentive program discussed at the beginning of the Six Sigma initiative?
21. What are the consequences for champions not helping and driving black belts?

All these questions are highly relevant and thought-provoking. And all your answers must be true and backed up by proof, not assumptions, to keep the momentum going.

The last question is directed at you, specifically, as a manager. You need to honestly examine whether or not you're removing barriers and supporting black belts in their efforts to achieve financial results. If you're not, then you need to take the necessary steps to do so. Remember: black belts and project teams see you as the motivating force, the initiator of the culture change required to identify and remove defects!

(Source: *Six Sigma for Managers*, by Greg Brue, New York: McGraw-Hill, 2002)

DFSS, like all of Six Sigma, is an active and pervasive methodology. Sustaining the initiative takes commitment at all levels and leadership from the top. Managers at all levels must be constantly striving to reinforce its value while introducing it further and further down the line to other employees, to *sustain the gain.*

Organizational Culture

Sustaining the DFSS initiative is not just a matter of leadership, support, and guidance from the top of the organization. A lot of the success of any DFSS initiative will depend on the culture of the organization.

You cannot change the culture of your organization by mandate. You start bringing about changes through the results of your DFSS projects. When your projects deliver results, everyone who participates in the projects or benefits from the results will appreciate the power of DFSS. As your organization experiences success after success, the culture will change.

Culture: Characteristics and Behavior

Six Sigma and DFSS are more than an approach and a set of tools. They generate a cultural change within an organization. They transform attitudes and mentalities.

More than a half century ago, English author H.G. Wells said, "Statistical thinking will one day be as necessary for efficient citizenship as the ability to read and write." It's likely that he meant something that we would now label more generally as "numerical literacy" or "numeracy."

But we can certainly agree with that prescient statement about statistical thinking as we now understand the term: "Statistical thinking" is a philosophy of learning and action based on the following fundamental principles:

- All work occurs in a system of interconnected processes.
- Variation exists in all processes.
- Understanding and reducing variation are keys to success.
(*Glossary and Tables for Statistical Quality Control,* 3rd edition, Milwaukee, WI: ASQ Quality Press, 1996)

How important is organizational culture? Consider the situation at GE under Welch—commonly cited as one of the top success stories for Six Sigma and Design for Six Sigma.

Success did not come quickly—and it did not come from simply implementing Six Sigma and DFSS. It came through preparation and initiatives that transformed thinking and attitudes.

Welch went through several stages at GE:

- In the 1980s, he focused on eliminating variety in GE's portfolio of businesses, which meant reducing the business units that were not meeting performance expectations, in a push to either be tops in every market or not compete in it.
- From the late 1980s to the mid-1990s, he focused on sim-

Six Sigma for One and All

Who should be trained in Six Sigma? According to GE, every employee:

All GE employees are trained in the strategy, statistical tools, and techniques of Six Sigma quality. People create results. Involving all employees is essential to GE's quality approach. GE is committed to providing opportunities and incentives for employees to focus their talents and energies on satisfying customers.

—General Electric Web site

plifying and eliminating activities that were not adding value, through Work-Outs and the Change Action Process, in a push to find better ways to do everything and to break down functional boundaries within the company.

- It wasn't until 1995 that he started using Six Sigma and then DFSS to focus on eliminating variation from business operations.

So, GE was prepared, operationally and culturally, for Six Sigma.

GE's experience and results would indicate it's worth striving for more training for employees, more black belts and green belts, and more employees on project teams.

Training

When you start Six Sigma, you focus on training black belts, since they're the tactical leaders of every project. When you start out, the ratio of black belts to green belts is about one to three. However, after the first year, about 10% of your employees are green belts.

That increase comes through training, to some extent, of course. But it also comes through expanding projects and providing opportunities to develop expertise on projects. In addition, as noted above, knowledge transfer, both structured and informal, promotes the spread of information throughout the organization. As black belts and green belts become more proficient, they reach out to train others. The exponential benefit is impressive; you must keep the momentum alive by fully recognizing and maximizing the power of this new resource by putting the black belts and green belts to work on new projects.

As you assign black belts and green belts to design projects, you will be involving other managers and employees in the Six Sigma initiative. It's natural, then, to provide green belt and black belt training to more and more employees. Training in DFSS methods and tools should be a logical extension of the general Six Sigma training.

Rewards and Recognition

One way to keep "converting" employees and managers to the benefits of DFSS is to implement recognition and rewards. It's idealistic to think that employees will support and promote DFSS simply because it's a way to satisfy the customers and to make bigger profits. After all, how many CEOs would buy that line? They'd expect to share in the financial gain of any initiative in which they've participated. The same is true of employees. They expect and deserve recognition and, of course, rewards.

Rewards can take the form of advancement. For example, choose master black belt and black belt candidates from among your top performers and make DFSS a path to promotion and managerial advancement for managers who are in charge of motivating people.

Another reward to offer is a compensation plan. To cover the full scope of DFSS activities, create compensation plans and progression plans for a full two years.

All Aboard!

To engage everyone throughout the organization in DFSS, you could do as Jack Welch did at GE for Six Sigma. To establish Six Sigma, Jack Welch made the following statements:

1. To get promoted, you must be Six Sigma trained.
2. 40% of top management bonuses are tied to Six Sigma goals.
3. Stock options are tied to Six Sigma performance.

As a result of this and other measures, GE had few problems engaging managers and employees in its Six Sigma initiative.

Recognition Pays

Smart Managing

When you publicly acknowledge the efforts and the success of black belts and their team members, you acknowledge that investing in DFSS has paid off both for the organization and for individuals. Recognition events emphasize the impact, relevance, and financial benefits of DFSS projects.

Depending on the size of your organization and the culture, these certification events can take the form of awards, percentage bonuses, or other incentive packages. They can range from lavish and elaborate banquets to more simple incentive programs. But whatever the form of recognition, when you emphasize the results achieved, the black belt reward structure inspires others to attain black belt status. Certification events are highly motivating public relations tools that really promote each individual success.

Since black belts are the primary players in a DFSS initiative, it makes good business sense to recognize their accomplishments formally and properly. As they meet or exceed their individual objectives, you must celebrate their successes, along with the results for the organization.

By hosting certification events, you send a clear signal that black belts and their efforts are highly valued. It's essential to do so—no matter what the individual rank, the project scope, or the dollar value realized, you must show that you appreciate their work and their successes. This recognition fosters a positive and supportive atmosphere, of course, but it also shows how seriously you take the DFSS initiative.

In addition to rewarding your black belts, it's important to retain them, especially because what they've been doing for your organization may attract the attention of other organizations.

As an aid to retaining black belts, consider hosting certification events that reward and recognize black belt achievements. To ensure continued support, develop compensation/incentive plans that include not just black belts and team members but also upper management.

If at all possible, you want to avoid a "brain drain" of your Six Sigma personnel. Obviously, people's circumstances can

Spread the Word

ITT Industries, Inc. recognizes and rewards team accomplishments through local recognition programs, a best practice symposium, and a software tracking tool. These practices also allow information to be shared. Vince Fayad, ITT's director of Value-Based Six Sigma, cites the company's recognition and rewards program as one of the six best practices at ITT that make the Six Sigma program successful (*Industry Week* online, April 1, 2002): "It's kind of knowledge management, knowledge sharing, so that people are all of a sudden realizing that these improvements can be made elsewhere in the organization."

change as they get promoted or leave the company. However, you can minimize the losses through recognition programs. Rewarding master black belts, black belts, and green belts can generate sustained interest and energy. Consider implementing an incentive-based compensation plan for all those involved in Six Sigma. From executives to line workers, managers to support staff, the compensation plan is a proven tool for retention.

Into Every Area

To be most effective, DFSS should operate throughout your organization. Consultants and other experts can help with the start up, but people at every level of the organization must take ownership of Six Sigma.

It seems that people tend to think more about using DFSS for products than for services; similarly they think about using DFSS for services more than for processes. If either of these scenarios applies to the conventional wisdom within your company, it is time to spread DFSS into other areas.

Any process can be represented as a set of inputs that generates a set of outputs. That process could be making a product or providing a service or connecting two areas of the organization.

Put simply, a process is a process, whatever the purpose or the function or the organization:

- Every process has inputs and outputs.
- Every process has suppliers and customers.

- Every process exhibits variation.

Since the purpose of DFSS is to design processes in order to make them function better, faster, and at less expense, DFSS can be applied to every process. That logic may seem a little idealistic to many managers—especially those who have witnessed other business ideologies pushed to extremes. Traditionally, transactional processes such **as sales** have benefited less than manufacturing from scientific methods. Therefore, the need for the structured and systematic methodology of DFSS is even greater—as is the opportunity for competitive advantages.

Consider this comment by Bob Galvin, former president and CEO of Motorola: "The lack of initial Six Sigma emphasis in the non-manufacturing areas was a mistake that cost Motorola at least \$5 billion over a four-year period."

It may not be enough to achieve six sigma with your products but remain at only three or four sigma with your

Product or Service or Process

Smart Managing

Jay Arthur, CEO of KnowWare International, makes the case for universal application of Six Sigma quite succinctly ("Six Sigma and Service vs. Manufacturing"):

I have found that, at an abstract level, there's no real difference between a service process and a manufacturing one. They both encounter delays, defects, and costs. One may produce purchase orders instead of computers, bills instead of brake liners, but they all take time, cost money, create defects, cause rework, and create waste. When we focus on finding the few key measures of defects, delay, and cost that are hampering profits and productivity, breakthrough improvements are easy.

Every aspect of your business follows a process; it may be a highly refined process or an error-prone, ad hoc one. Regardless of whether it's service or manufacturing, there are always defects in the process steps, delays between steps, and increased costs involved in reworking or scrapping some work product.

As for the claim that Six Sigma works for products but not for services or processes, Arthur dismisses it categorically: "Nothing could be further from the truth. This is just a convenient way for crafty employees to dodge learning the improvement strategies."

> ### Let the Figures Make Your Case
>
> If anybody suggests that Six Sigma is for manufacturing only, just show the following figures from the *Quality Digest* 2003 Six Sigma Survey. This is how the respondents reported that DFSS was used in the following functional areas of their organizations:
>
> | | |
> |---|---|
> | manufacturing 520 | purchasing 256 |
> | plant operations 357 | shipping/receiving 240 |
> | engineering 349 | sales 207 |
> | customer service 311 | research/development 193 |
> | test inspection 303 | document control 190 |
> | administration 300 | pollution prevention 100 |
>
> A survey by DynCorp showed the following breakdown of companies using Six Sigma:
>
> | | |
> |---|---|
> | manufacturing companies 49.3% | other companies 12.5% |
> | service companies 38.2% | |

services. We commonly hear comments like "That company has a great product, but it's sure difficult to do business with them!"

Jack Welch mandated Six Sigma in all areas of GE, including transactional processes. In his comments in the 1997 GE Annual Report, he made the following statement:

> Six Sigma is quickly becoming part of the genetic code of our future leadership. Six Sigma training is now an ironclad prerequisite for promotion to any professional or managerial position in the Company—and a requirement for any award of stock options.

Processes Depend on People

While DFSS may be initiated from the top, it works because of the employees on the project teams. Thus, managers at all levels should be focused on this big question—"How can we keep employees energized on DFSS?"

The following strategies may help, as suggested by Zack Swinney, a quality auditor and author of a dozen articles on quality, in "Keep Employees Energized on Quality" (www.isixsigma.com/library/content/c001112a.asp):

- **Break ties with the past.** Help employees understand that the current processes are not necessarily the best ways to do business and that we can improve through a greater focus on the customers, quality techniques and tools, and technology.
- **Reward as a team.** If you want employees to work as a team, you must recognize and reward them as a team.
- **Take breaks.** Without breaks, employees can burn out or lose their ability to focus on details. It's not time on a job that matters, but results. And encourage exercise: we're all healthier, both physically and mentally, when we get some exercise. Also, breaks and exercise can help promote creativity.
- **Have fun.** DFSS is serious work, but that doesn't mean that members of a project can't have fun and enjoy working together.
- **Think big picture.** Employees can become so engrossed in the details of applying DFSS that they forget the larger

---

Include the Subcontractors

For Example

Pratt & Whitney, a company that designs and manufactures engines for aircraft and space propulsion and power systems, decided to stop having a subcontractor provide advance part prototypes, because the subcontractor used processes different from those used at P&W—even though the subcontractor could react faster to design changes than in-house production teams.

The company first adopted a policy of doing all advance technology prototypes in-house, so it could put the production process in place at the same time.

Although that policy eliminated the problems of discontinuity for parts that P&W would make in-house, there were still problems of discontinuity for parts that would be supplied by subcontractors, because of process differences. P&W decided to select sole source subcontractors and involve them in the design process from the beginning, so the companies would design parts together and develop processes that would be compatible.

picture. Managers, master black belts, and black belts need to remind the team members of the project objectives and the purposes for using DFSS.

Expanding DFSS Beyond the Organization

Organizations that want to improve their products and processes should involve everyone upstream and downstream in the value chain of their customers, to improve everything incorporated into their products or services. That means involving suppliers, contractors, outsource partners, and distributors.

Work with these members of the value chain to improve their products and processes. Establish a common language and standard metrics, share your expectations of quality, and help develop attitudes of excellence among all people who are linked in the value chain. If other contributors to the chain are not involved in improving quality as an extension of the DFSS initiatives, you cannot hope to be providing the best quality in your products and services.

DFSS Means Six Sigma from Suppliers

A major appliance manufacturer had a chronic problem with a supplier. The agitators for its washing machines routinely did not fit. As a result, inserting the agitator into the machine, which should have been a task for one employee, would require two employees and some force. Even then, the washing machines would often function poorly. Field technicians were unable to fix the problem, so the machines had to return to the plant. This problem cost the company $1 million annually.

The black belt assigned to the problem examined the agitators and determined that they varied in weight—and that the supplier never weighed the agitators!

The company then involved the supplier in its quality process. The supplier examined its 10 injection molds, identified those that were causing the variation in weight, and then corrected the problem, so that all agitators were of the correct weight.

The moral of the story: DFSS initiatives start at the beginning— even if that means going beyond the walls to the source.

Make your suppliers a part of your Six Sigma world. You want them involved in your initiative because, depending on your industry, if you're engaged in making or servicing something, chances are good that you use their parts or processes to complete it. Obviously, they affect your defect levels and waste streams.

Basically, you want to train them and get them up to speed with Six Sigma so they can fix or eliminate defects before they reach you. You can leverage both Six Sigma standards and your supplier relationships to further effective, positive, and lasting change in this area. It's in the best interests of your top 10 suppliers to conform to your new standard of quality—not only to retain your business, but also to actually improve their own simply by embracing the core attributes of Six Sigma.

Manager's Checklist for Chapter 9

❑ Six Sigma planning should be built into the business plan; it should be considered an integral element of any strategic planning.

❑ Establish a good and extensive communication plan, both externally and internally, and maintain it to keep everybody current on your Six Sigma initiative. Use company meetings, newsletters, e-mail, or any other appropriate vehicle to keep people aware of activities and results and interested in the DFSS initiative.

❑ Support continual training programs for DFSS and Six Sigma, throughout the organization, both formally and informally.

❑ Institute a pay-for-performance incentive plan. Linking a bonus structure to DFSS project outcomes will help promote the methodology throughout the organization.

❑ Host specific black belt certification events, to show support for DFSS and recognition for key contributors.

❑ Involve your key suppliers in your DFSS initiative. Partner to extend the improvement efforts the length of the value chain.

❏ Be sure senior executives visibly support DFSS and its strategic importance with regular reviews.

❏ Maintain a DFSS sustainability checklist. This is an excellent tool for measuring the health of your initiative over time.

Index

A

Absence of trust, 96
Accountability, 23–24, 96
Accuracy of metrics, 124
Adjourning stage of teams, 95
Adsit, Dennis, 23
Affinity diagrams, 40, 41, 127
Akao, Yoji, 127
American Productivity & Quality
    Center, 71
The Analytic Hierarchy Process,
    133
Analytic Hierarchy Process
    (AHP), 132–133
Anticipatory Failure
    Determination (AFD), 49, 50,
    147–148
Antis, David Jr., 30, 121, 132,
    162
Arthur, Jay, 177
Ashby, Michael F., 45
Attendance matrix, 36
Automotive Industry Action
    Group, 125
Averages, overemphasizing,
    61–62, 72–73
Avoidance of accountability, 96

B

Bad metrics, 78
Baselines, 67, 68
Basic requirements, in Kano
    model, 128

Bell curves, 74
Belts, varying Six Sigma systems,
    92
Benchmarking
    elements of, 68–71, 123
    limitations for DFSS, 43
    using metrics for, 67
Benchmarking Code of Conduct,
    71
Benefits, quantifying, 8
Berthiez, Gwendolyn, 117
Best practices, 116
Bias, 65, 124
Black belts
    certification, 91
    champions trained as, 85
    common mistakes, 112–113
    continuing to train, 173–174
    defined, 36
    qualifications and responsibili-
        ties, 34–35, 88 90
    recognition and rewards for,
        175
    selecting, 110
    team building role, 94–95
Bonuses for Six Sigma imple-
    mentation, 97, 174–175
Books, suggested, 99–101, 162
Breaks, encouraging, 179
Business metrics, 55
Business plans, DFSS projects in,
    169

C

Capability index (Cp), 48, 76, 150–151
Capability index (Cpk), 48, 76, 150
Capability ratio (Cr), 48, 151
Carmichael, Ronald, 117
Carnell, Mike, 112
Cavanagh, Roland R., 44
CDOV, 30–31
Centering process capability and performance, 150, 151, 152
Certification events, 175
Certification processes, 116
Champions
    common mistakes of, 113–115
    credibility, 35
    defined, 34
    DFSS implementation role, 106–110
    qualifications and responsibilities, 34, 84–86
    training all leaders as, 115–116
Change, 31, 117
Charters, 37
Charts, 67
Chatterjee, Ritesh, 115
Chief executive officer (CEO), 82–84, 104–106
Chowdhury, Subir, 25
Cisco Systems, 17
Classroom training, 12. *See also* Training
Cluster sampling, 153
Commitment
    essential for leaders, 7, 12, 115
    maximizing, 118, 178–180
    teams' lack of, 96
Common causes, 150
Communication plans, 39, 168
Compensation, tying DFSS results to, 96–97, 118, 174–175, 176

Competitive advantages, 22–24
Competitive benchmarking, 69, 123
Competitors, tearing down products of, 71
Complacency, avoiding, 164–166
Concept designs, 46
Concept screening, 134
Concurrent processes, 15–16
Confidence, required of CEOs, 83
Conflict, 95, 96
Conjoint analysis, 40
Consultants, 97–98, 116
Contextual inquiry, 40, 126
Control charts, 161
Control limits, 76
Control plans, 160–161
Cooper, Robert G., 4
Cost factors
    basic role in DFSS, 19–22
    combining with time and quality, 16–17
    design for, 140
    linking metrics to, 66
Cost of poor quality, 20–21
Cost savings from DFSS, 21–22
Credibility of champions, 35
Creveling, Clyde M., 30, 121, 132, 162
Critical thinking, 62–64
Critical-to-process metrics (CTPs), 43–44
Critical-to-quality characteristics (CTQs)
    comparing to technical requirements, 46
    defined, 9
    as DFSS focus, 16–17
    documenting, 42–43
    as guide to metrics, 56–57
    identifying and prioritizing, 42
Cross-functional teams, 11, 15–16

CTQ flowdowns, 30, 31
CTx's, 17
Culture. *See* Organizational cul-
   ture
Culture of accountability, 23–24
Customer needs
   as DFSS focus, 10, 16–17
   as guide to metrics, 56–57
   identifying and prioritizing,
      40–42
   types of, 56
Customer quality, 45
Customers
   defining, 39
   keeping involved in processes,
      166–167
   viewing as partners, 118
Customer service, 21
Customer survey analysis, 126
Cyclical variations, 153

D
Damage mode(s) and effects
   analysis (DMEA), 146
Data collection, objectives for, 37
Defects
   as basic Six Sigma focus, 2
   defined, 59
   mistakes versus, 149
   overemphasizing, 60–61
Defects per million opportunities
   (DPMO), 2–3, 59–60
Delegation, 106
Delights, 56
Demanded Quality Hierarchy,
   130
Denominator management, 60
Deployment, 106
Design concepts, selecting, 43
Design failure mode(s) and
   effects analysis (DFMEA), 146
Design for Assembly (DFA), 139

Design for Cost (DFC), 140
Design for Environment (DFE),
   141
Design for Green (DFG), 141
Design for International (DFI), 141
Design for Manufacture and
   Assembly (DFMA), 10–11,
   139
Design for Manufacture (DFM),
   139
Design for Reliability (DFR), 140
Design for Serviceability/Service
   (DFS), 140–141
Design for Six Sigma (DFSS)
   anticipating change when
      implementing, 31
   applying beyond organization,
      180–181
   applying to all processes,
      176–180
   causes of failure, 112–115, 168
   competitive advantages, 22–24
   cost, time, and quality focus,
      17–22
   customer role, 16–17
   marketing basics, 10
   misconceptions about, 10–12
   more than tools, 24–26
   origins, 8–9
   overview of key players, 81–82
   reducing failure rate with,
      15–16
   Six Sigma versus, 4–8, 54
   variations on basic approach,
      28–31
Design for Six Sigma (book), 25
*Design for Six Sigma in
   Technology and Product
   Development*, 30, 121, 162
Design for Testability (DFT), 140
Design for X assessments, 48–49,
   138–141

Design of Experiments (DOE), 10–11, 154–157
Design phase, 32, 46–49
Design Planning Table, 131
Detectability, rating failures by, 146
Determination, required of CEOs, 83
DFSS. *See* Design for Six Sigma (DFSS)
Discrimination, 65, 124
Dysfunctional teams, 96

E
Elevator speech, 5
EMC Corp., 17
Employee development metrics, 58
Employees. *See also* Teams
  benefits of DFSS for, 24
  keeping energized for DFSS, 178–180
  retaining, 118–119, 175–176
Engineering analyses, 45
Engineering models, 29
Entitlements, baselines versus, 68
Environmentally conscious design, 141
Error proofing, 45, 148–149
Estimated sigma, 150
Estimating resources, 109
Evolutionary operations (EVOP), 50
Evolutionary stages of teams, 94–95
Excitement attributes, 128
Executives. *See* Chief executive officer (CEO); Leadership; Management
Expectations
  adjusting, 108
  of customers, 56
  of DFSS, 24–25

F
Failure Modes and Effects Analysis (FMEA)
  AFD versus, 147
  customer priorities and, 42
  developing control plans from, 161
  elements of, 143–146
  in Optimize phase, 49
  using with Pugh technique, 46, 134
Failure of DFSS, 112–115
Failure of new products and services, 14–16
Fayad, Vince, 116, 176
Fear of conflict, 96
Financial goals, linking metrics to, 66
Financial returns, validating, 117
Fisher, Ronald, 154
The Five Dysfunctions of a Team, 96
Five-step processes, 1–2, 6–7
FMEA. *See* Failure Modes and Effects Analysis (FMEA)
Forming stage, 94
Fractional experiments, 156
Freezing requirements, 109
Full factorial experiments, 156
Functional benchmarking, 69, 123

G
Galvin, Bob, 177
Gap analyses, 6, 48, 71–72
GE Medical Systems, 19
General Electric
  preparing culture for Six Sigma, 172–173
  Six Sigma results tied to compensation, 97, 174
  transactional process applications for Six Sigma, 178

Generic design process, 30
Good, defining, 17
Granta Design software, 45
Green belts
    common mistakes, 112–113
    continuing to train, 173–174
    qualifications and responsibili-
        ties, 35–36, 90–92

H
Half-fraction experiments, 156
Harry, Mikel J., 104, 105
Hipple, Jack, 147–148
House of quality (HOQ), 129–131
Huber, Charles, 109

I
I^{2}DOV, 30
IBM, 17
Ideal function, 159
Identify phase, 32, 39–46
IDOV method
    Design phase, 32, 46–49
    Identify phase, 32, 39–46
    Optimize phase, 32, 49–51
    overview, 32–33
    Plan/Prerequisites phase, 32,
        33–39
    Verify/Validate phase, 32,
        51–52
Implementation
    causes of failure, 112–115
    champions' role, 106–110
    lessons learned, 117–119
    long-term, 76–77, 165
    management role, 104–108
    obstacles, 111–112, 168
    overall recommendations,
        115–117
Improvement goals, 37
Inattention to results, 96
Infrastructure support for DFSS,
    169–170

Innova 2000, 19
Innovation, promoting, 44
Intangible benefits of DFSS,
    23–24
Integrity, required of CEOs, 83
Interactive prototyping, 41
Internal benchmarking, 69, 123
Internal processes
    applying DFSS to all, 176–180
    benchmarking for, 69
    metrics for, 58
International Benchmarking
    Clearinghouse, 71
International Quality Federation,
    91
Interrelationship digraphs, 49
Introduction to Six Sigma, 111
Ishikawa, Kaoru, 17
ITT Industries, 176

J
Just-in-time training, 36

K
Kano model, 40–41, 127–128
Key process input variables
    (KPIVs), 153
Key process output variables
    (KPOVs), 153
Key process variables (KPVs), 39
King, Bob, 132
KJ method, 41, 127
Knowledge management, 167
Knowledge transfer tools, 107,
    167–168
Kotter, John, 84

L
Lack of team commitment, 96
Launsby, Robert, 109
Leadership. *See also* Chief execu-
    tive officer (CEO); Manage-
    ment

Leadership (*Continued*)
  critical thinking by, 63–64
  importance to implementation,
    104–106
  importance to sustaining gains,
    168–169
  involvement in setting metrics,
    67
Leading Change, 84
Leaning into Six Sigma, 112
Lencioni, Patrick, 96
Lessons learned databases, 167
Lewis, John, 117
Life cycle costs, reducing, 19–20
Linearity of measurements, 65,
  124
Living with the customer, 126
Long-term dynamic mean varia-
  tion, 77, 165
Lower control limit, 76
Lower specification limit, 75
Lusmanoff, Antone, 117

M
Mahna, Ritesh, 111
Management. *See also* Chief
  executive officer (CEO)
  common mistakes, 113–115
  critical thinking by, 63–64
  DFSS implementation role,
    104–108, 169–171
  importance of support to
    DFSS, 7, 12
  involvement in setting metrics,
    67
  overall recommendations for,
    115–117
Mapping, 38–39
Master black belts, 86–88,
  112–113
Material selection, 45
*Materials Selection in Mechanical
  Design*, 45

McKinnon, Tanicka L., 111
Mean, 72–73
Measurement. *See* Metrics
Measurement system analysis
  (MSA)
  defined, 39, 65
  elements of, 123–125
  at planning stage, 38
Median, 73
Metrics
  applying critical thinking to,
    62–64
  bad, 78
  basic importance and guide-
    lines, 54–56
  basic steps in setting, 66–72
  checklist for, 78–79
  for CTQ, 43
  as part of project objectives,
    37, 38
  reliability and validity, 64–65,
    123, 140
  standards for, 58–62
  throughout organization, 118
  variation and standard devia-
    tion in, 72–78
  what to measure, 56–58
Misconceptions about DFSS,
  10–12
Mistakes, defects versus, 149
Mizuno, Shigeru, 127
Mode, 73
Modeling, 47
Monte Carlo simulation, 157–158
Motorola
  delays in applying Six Sigma
    to all processes, 177
  origins of Six Sigma terminolo-
    gy with, 91
  shift calculations, 77
Multi-vari analysis, 152–153

N
Neuman, Robert P., 44
Nonconformance, 3
Non-critical metrics, 57
Normal curve, 74
Normal variation, 75
Norming stage, 95

O
Objectives, 37–38, 55
One-sigma processes, 2
Opportunities, 59
Optimize phase, 32, 49–51
Organizational culture
    DFSS impact on, 23–24, 31
    sustaining DFSS gains in,
        171–176
Orthogonal arrays, 154–155, 159

P
PACCAR Inc., 18
Pande, Peter S., 44
Parallel processes, 15–16
Parnella, Jim, 5
Part planning (HOQ), 131
Past, breaking with, 179
Patience, required of CEOs, 83
P-diagram, 159
Performance index (Pp), 48, 152
Performance index (Ppk), 48,
    151–152
Performance ratio (Pr), 48, 152
Performance specifications, as
    DFSS focus, 8–9
Performing stage, 95
Phase-gate reviews
    defined, 32
    in IDOV method, 33
    recommendations for effective-
        ness, 121–122
    responsibility for, 107–108
    scheduling, 38
Plan/Prerequisites phase, 32,
    33–39

Poka-Yoke, 148–149
Portal technology for knowledge
    transfer, 107, 167
Positional variations, 153
Pratt & Whitney, 179
Precision of metrics, 124
Prioritizing customer require-
    ments, 41–42
Process capability
    identifying data in planning
        stage, 38
    measures of, 48, 75–76,
        149–152
    preserving, 166
    short- versus long-term, 77,
        165
Processes, applying DFSS to all,
    176–180
Process failure mode(s) and
    effects analysis (PFMEA), 146
Process maps, 38–39
Process performance metrics, 48,
    151–152
Process planning (HOQ), 131
Process width, 75, 76
Production/delivery quality, 45
Production planning (HOQ), 131
Product planning (HOQ), 131
Products, reason for failure,
    14–16
Product teardowns, 71
Profitability, 8, 117
Project charters, 37
Project objectives, 37–38
Project reviews, 32. *See also*
    Phase-gate reviews
Project selection, 33
Pugh concept selection tech-
    nique, 43, 44, 46, 134–138
Pyzdek, Thomas, 25, 60, 93,
    121, 162

Q

Quadratic loss function, 159
Quality, types of, 45
Quality Characteristics Hierarchy, 130
Quality factors, 16–18
Quality function deployment (QFD)
  as alternative to baselines, 68
  common mistakes, 131–132
  described, 41
  selected tools, 127–133
  when to use, 42, 57
Quality Planning Table, 131
Quantifying benefits, 8
Quarter-fraction experiments, 156

R

Random sampling, 153
Range, 73, 74
Rating systems, for black belt candidates, 90
Recognition and rewards, 95–97, 174–176
Reference checking for consultants, 97
Relationships matrix, 130
Reliability and validity, 64–65, 123, 140
Repeatability of measurements, 65, 124
Reproducibility of measurements, 65, 124
Requirements
  customer expectations as, 57
  freezing, 109
Requirements flowdown, 9
Resources, estimating, 109
Response surface methodology (RSM), 50, 51, 156–157
Responsiveness of metrics, 67

Results, inattention to, 96
Retention, 118–119, 175–176
Return on training investment, 116
Reviews. See Project reviews
Rewards. See Recognition and rewards
Risk analysis, 45
Robust design strategy, 50, 158–159
Root-sum-square analysis, 48

S

Saaty, Thomas L., 133
Sampling, 153
Schurr, Stefan, 132
Scorecards
  balancing, 57–58
  creating, 43
  elements and functions of, 133–134, 135
  populating in Design phase, 47
Scoring, in Pugh concept selection technique, 138
Senior reviews, 98
Serial processes, 15
Serviceability, design for, 140–141
Service failure mode(s) and effects analysis (SFMEA), 146
Services
  applying DFSS to, 176–180
  reason for failure, 14–16
Severity, rating failures by, 145, 146
Seward, Brian, 111
Shift, 76–77, 165
Shingo, Shigeo, 148
Sigma, defined, 2
Sigma levels, 2–3, 20
Sigma of the individuals, 151
Signal-to-noise ratio, 159

Significance of variations, 79
Simplicity of metrics, 67
Simplification, 22
Simulation, Monte Carlo, 157–158
SIPOC analysis, 145
Six Sigma
  basic benefits, 25
  current popularity, 23
  Design for Six Sigma versus, 4–8, 54
  method overview, 1–4
  tying results to compensation, 97, 174–175, 176
Six Sigma and Beyond, 3
The Six Sigma Handbook, 121, 162
The Six Sigma Project Planner, 60, 93, 121, 162
Six Sigma shift, 76–77, 165
The Six Sigma Way, 44
Slutsky, Jeffrey Lee, 30, 121, 132, 162
SMART metrics, 64
SMART objectives, 38
Smith, Craig T., 132
Software failure mode(s) and effects analysis (SFMEA), 146
Software for knowledge transfer, 107, 167
Special causes, 150
Specifications
  creating, 42–43
  freezing, 109
  limits, 74
Spider diagrams, 49
Sponsors. See Champions
Spread, 151
Stability of measurements, 65, 124
Stamatis, D. H., 3
Standard deviation, 2, 59, 74

Standards for metrics, 58–62
Statistical process control (SPC), 52, 72–76. See also Process capability
Statistical thinking, 172
Statistics
  basic role in DFSS, 11
  training valuable for black belts, 88, 89
  variation and standard deviation, 72–78
Storming stage, 95
Stratified sampling, 153
Subcontractors, involving in DFSS, 179
Subgroup sampling, 153
"Successful Six Sigma Project Reviews," 121–122
Suggested readings, 99–101, 162
Suppliers as partners, 118, 179, 180–181
Survey analysis, 126
Sustainability checklist, 170–171
Swinney, Zack, 178
Systematic sampling, 153
System failure mode(s) and effects analysis (SFMEA), 146
Systems engineering, 8–9

T
Taguchi methods, 158–159
Target tolerances, 47–48
Team members
  responsibilities, 36, 92–93
  selecting, 110
Teams
  evolutionary stages, 94–95
  five dysfunctions, 96
  recognition and rewards for, 95–97, 179
  selecting, 110
Temporal variations, 153

Testability, 140
Three-sigma processes, 2–3
Time factors, 16–19
Time off, encouraging, 179
Tolerance, 160
Tolerance design, 47–48, 160
Tools
  Analytic Hierarchy Process,
    132–133
  Anticipatory Failure
    Determination, 49, 50,
    147–148
  benchmarking, 43, 67, 68–71,
    123
  control plans, 160–161
  Design for X, 48–49, 138–141
  Failure Modes and Effects
    Analysis, 143–146 (see also
    Failure Modes and Effects
    Analysis [FMEA])
  measurement system analysis,
    38, 39, 65, 123–125
  Monte Carlo simulation,
    157–158
  multi-vari analysis, 152–153
  phase-gate reviews, 121–122
    (see also Phase-gate
    reviews)
  Poka-Yoke, 148–149
  process capability and per-
    formance studies, 149–152
    (see also Process capability)
  Pugh concept selection tech-
    nique, 43, 44, 46, 134–138
  quality function deployment,
    127–132 (see also Quality
    function deployment [QFD])
  robust design strategy, 50,
    158–159
  scorecards, 133–134, 135 (see
    also Scorecards)
  tolerance design, 47–48, 160

voice of the customer, 6,
    16–17, 40–41, 125–127
Total Design, 134–136
Training
  for black belts, 88, 89,
    173–174
  for CEOs and other executives,
    82, 104
  for champions, 85, 115–116
  effective, 12
  for green belts, 173–174
  just-in-time, 36
  for master black belts, 87
  return on investment, 116
  to sustain DFSS gains,
    173–174
  team members, 93
Transactional processes, 178
Transfer functions, 29, 47
Treichler, David, 117
TRIZ method, 44
Trust, 96
Tuckman, Bruce, 94
21-question status check,
    170–171

U
Upper control limit, 76
Upper specification limit, 75

V
Validity and reliability, 64–65,
    123, 140
Variable requirements, in Kano
    model, 128
Variations
  averages versus, 61–62
  measurement parameters for,
    65
  in process capability and per-
    formance, 48, 149–153
  robustness and, 50, 158–159
  shift and, 76–77, 165

significance, 79
statistical concepts, 72–75
Vendors as partners, 118
Verify/Validate phase, 32, 51–52
Vision, 105, 168–169
Visual displays of metrics, 67
Voice of the customer (VOC)
as DFSS focus, 16–17
incorporating into product
development, 6
selected tools, 40–41, 125–127
Voice of the customer table, 42,
128–129, 130

W
Wants, needs versus, 56
Waxer, Charles, 121–122
Web sites
American Productivity &
Quality Center, 71

International Quality
Federation, 91
Introduction to Six Sigma, 111
Six Sigma deployment failures,
112
Six Sigma management tips,
115
"Successful Six Sigma Project
Reviews," 121
Welch, Jack, 83, 172–173, 178
White belts, 92
Winning at New Products, 4
World markets, design for, 141

Y
Yamada Electric, 148
Yellow belts, 92

Z
Zero Quality Control (ZQC) system, 149